MONOGRAPHS OF THE
SOCIETY FOR RESEARCH IN
CHILD DEVELOPMENT

Serial No. 235, Vol. 58, No. 7, 1993

· 13672 (7281) Ear.

EARLY SUPPLEMENTARY
FEEDING AND COGNITION:
EFFECTS OVER TWO DECADES

Ernesto Pollitt
Kathleen S. Gorman
Patrice L. Engle
Reynaldo Martorell
Juan Rivera

WITH COMMENTARIES BY
Theodore D. Wachs
Nevin S. Scrimshaw

AND A REPLY BY THE AUTHORS

MONOGRAPHS OF THE SOCIETY FOR RESEARCH IN CHILD DEVELOPMENT
Serial No. 235, Vol. 58, No. 7, 1993

CONTENTS

ABSTRACT   v

I. INTRODUCTION   1

II. METHODOLOGY AND FINDINGS OF
THE LONGITUDINAL STUDY   7

III. CONCEPTUAL RATIONALE FOR THE FOLLOW-UP   20

IV. METHODOLOGICAL AND
SUBSTANTIVE CONSIDERATIONS   26

V. METHODS OF THE CROSS-SECTIONAL FOLLOW-UP   39

VI. RESULTS FROM THE CROSS-SECTIONAL FOLLOW-UP   56

VII. DISCUSSION   74

APPENDIX A:
AVERAGE NUTRIENT INTAKES
OF ATOLE AND FRESCO SUBJECTS   86

APPENDIX B:
DESCRIPTIONS OF TESTS USED IN THE
ANALYSIS OF THE PRESCHOOL BATTERY   88

REFERENCES   91

ACKNOWLEDGMENTS   99

COMMENTARIES

GOING BEYOND NUTRITION:
NUTRITION, CONTEXT, AND DEVELOPMENT
Theodore D. Wachs   100

EARLY SUPPLEMENTARY FEEDING AND COGNITION:
A RETROSPECTIVE COMMENT
Nevin S. Scrimshaw   111

REPLY

NUTRITION AND DEVELOPMENT:
CONSIDERATIONS FOR INTERVENTION
Ernesto Pollitt and Kathleen S. Gorman   116

CONTRIBUTORS 119

STATEMENT OF
EDITORIAL POLICY 121

ABSTRACT

POLLITT, ERNESTO; GORMAN, KATHLEEN S.; ENGLE, PATRICE L.; MARTORELL, REYNALDO; and RIVERA, JUAN. Early Supplementary Feeding and Cognition: Effects over Two Decades. With Commentaries by THEODORE D. WACHS and NEVIN S. SCRIMSHAW; and a Reply by ERNESTO POLLITT and KATHLEEN S. GORMAN. *Monographs of the Society for Research in Child Development*, 1993, **58**(7, Serial No. 235).

The study reported in this *Monograph* of the effects of early supplementary feeding on cognition included two data collection periods: a longitudinal investigation spanning the years 1969–1977 and a cross-sectional follow-up carried out in 1988–1989. The study was conducted in four rural villages in Guatemala and compared the differential effects of exposure in childhood (0–7 years) to an Atole supplement (11.5 g of protein; 163 kcal) or a Fresco supplement (59 kcal) on performance on a battery of psychoeducational and information-processing tests in adolescence and young adulthood (11–24 years). In this report, particular attention is given to a cohort of subjects who were exposed to the supplement prenatally and during at least the first 2 years of postnatal life. Data on this subsample are contrasted with those on a cohort of subjects who received the supplement only after 24 months of life. The *Monograph* also reports results from an analysis of the supplementation effects in infancy and early childhood.

Consistent differences between groups on the psychoeducational tests were observed. Adolescents from Atole villages scored significantly higher on tests of knowledge, numeracy, reading, and vocabulary than Fresco subjects. Atole was also associated with a faster reaction time in information-processing tasks. Significant interactions helped identify two groups who benefited more from the Atole treatment: those at the lowest levels of socioeconomic status and those who attained the highest levels of primary schooling. The consistent differences in test performance established in the follow-up assessment contrast sharply with the few and less pronounced between-group differences observed in the infancy and preschool periods.

After close scrutiny of alternative hypotheses, it is concluded that nutritional differences provide the strongest explanation for the test performance differences observed in the follow-up between the subjects exposed to the Atole and those exposed to the Fresco supplement.

This *Monograph* reports results from a study of the effects of supplementary feeding of newborn to 7-year-old children on their subsequent performance as adolescents and young adults (11–24 years) on a battery of psychoeducational and information-processing tests. The study, which began in 1969, was conducted in a nutritionally at-risk population in the Department of El Progreso, Eastern Guatemala. The intent was to test the hypothesis that protein deficiency in infants and children delays mental development.

We report the effects of the nutritional intervention on cognition during infancy, the preschool period, and, more extensively, adolescence and early adulthood. Issues of differential effects from pre- versus postnatal supplement are excluded; similarly, the current analyses do not attend to the possible differential effect of specific nutrients.

BACKGROUND

This section describes the key theoretical and research issues in international nutrition and in developmental biology and psychology that were dominant at the time the study was launched (1969). The discussion aims to justify the study design that was chosen and the research questions of concern here.

International Nutrition and the Protein Gap

Cicely Williams's (1933) description of kwashiorkor and her suggestion that its etiology could be found in a deficiency of "amino acids or protein" became a landmark; thereafter, protein deficiency became the object of intensive study and international concern.[1] For at least the following four decades, protein was considered to be the major limiting factor in the diets of most undernourished children in the less developed countries, particularly in Africa. Illustrative is the 1953 publication of an Expert Committee on Nutrition from the UN Food and Agricultural Organization and the World Health Organization (cited in McLaren, 1974). Without the necessary epidemiological data, it nevertheless stated that kwashiorkor was "the most serious and widespread nutritional disorder known to medical and nutritional sciences." Thus, it is not surprising that the United Nations instituted a Protein Advisory Group in 1955 and that groups of experts in international nutrition provided strong recommendations to develop local protein-rich foods. Moreover, evaluations of lysine fortification programs were also launched in target populations considered protein deficient (McLaren, 1974).

However, by the late 1950s and the early 1960s, it was becoming apparent that protein was not the sole growth-limiting factor among malnourished children. In 1959, Jelliffe coined the term "protein calorie deficiency" to encompass kwashiorkor, marasmus, and mild to moderate forms of protein calorie malnutrition.[2] In 1974, the head of the division of nutrition at the World Health Organization estimated that there were 98,470,000 children (0–4 years old) suffering from PEM in Asia, Africa, and Latin America (Bengoa, 1974).

PEM and Mental Development

The hypothesis linking PEM (protein energy malnutrition) to later cognitive deficit can be traced to the beginning of the twentieth century (see, e.g., Nicholls, 1923). Most of the research, however, was conducted during the mid-1950s (Geber & Dean, 1955, 1956) and the 1960s (Cabak & Najdanvic, 1965; Cravioto & Robles, 1965; Jelliffe, 1965; Pollitt & Granoff, 1967; Scrimshaw, 1969; Scrimshaw & Gordon, 1968; Stoch & Smythe, 1963). The published data extended clinical observations on malnourished children. Rich descriptions were provided of the behavioral apathy, listlessness, and reduced motor activity observed among severely undernourished children

[1] Kwashiorkor is the result of a protein-deficient diet. It is generally an acute condition that tends to occur at the end of the first or during the second year of life. Oedema, hypopigmentation or dermatoses, dyspigmentation of the hair, and a significant increment in the size of the liver are pathognomonic signs of protein deficiency.

[2] Marasmus is characterized by severe retardation in linear growth as the final stage in a long process of depletion due to a diet poor in quality and quantity. It often occurs during the first year of life, but it is also found among older children. Oedema is not present. The term "protein calorie malnutrition" was subsequently changed to "protein energy malnutrition" (PEM); we use the latter in this *Monograph*.

(Autret & Béhar, 1954; Jelliffe, 1965). Thus, it was only natural to suspect that undernutrition affected the brain since its effects on vital organs such as the liver had been well documented (McLaren, Faris, & Zekian, 1968).

Most, if not all, of the studies conducted during the 1960s on the effects of PEM on human behavior relied on correlational research designs. Investigators observed that infants and young children with a history of severe PEM (i.e., marasmus, kwashiorkor, or both) had poorer scores on developmental scales (e.g., the Bayley Scales), IQ tests, and tasks testing specific intellectual functions than comparison groups (for reviews, see Pollitt & Thomson, 1977; Ricciuti, 1981). Stunted children without clinical signs of severe malnutrition also performed comparatively poorly on tests of intersensory integration (Cravioto, DeLicardie, & Birch, 1966).

Inferences made at that time about the causal effects of PEM on cognition were thus based primarily on correlational data. Concerns regarding possible confounding and moderating effects of social and economic variables that covaried with nutritional status were dealt with by matched-group research designs. Subjects differing in anthropometry (e.g., above and below the tenth percentile for height distribution of the Harvard Growth Standards) were matched on an array of potential confounders (e.g., mother's education, father's occupation), and their performance on psychological tests (e.g., IQ) was compared (Cabak & Najdanvic, 1965; Hertzig, Birch, Richardson, & Tizard, 1972).

The consistency in findings among different studies did not compensate for the critical limitations of ex post facto research designs or for problems inherent to the nature of the research question. The social-psychological factors that characterized the immediate family environment of the PEM child were neither known nor controlled for. The factors that were controlled for were broad, graduated parameters of social structure such as mother's education or family income. Thus, conclusive inferences could not be drawn from such studies, no matter how carefully investigators matched the samples. In addition, operational definitions of nutritional status based on anthropometry are crude since body size is not determined solely by nutrient intake (Pollitt & Ricciuti, 1969; for an early, articulate discussion of this issue, see Suchman, 1968).

Although it was recognized at the time that laboratory studies conducted with experimental animals could make important contributions to understanding the problem, such studies also had serious limitations. Their focus was on severe protein deficiency, and the human conditions of mild to moderate malnutrition were not simulated in the laboratory. In addition, the animal models could not include social-environmental variables considered to be potential confounders or effect modifiers (Pollitt, 1969).

Recognition of the limitations in the designs of the studies conducted in this period led to an appreciation of the scientific merits of research protocols that included supplementary feeding as a key experimental variable. Shifting to this approach provided an opportunity to randomize study subjects and to control a substantive portion of a child's daily nutrient intake. It also allowed for the manipulation of the timing and duration of exposure to the experimental treatment and for a focus on mild to moderate PEM. During the 1960s, at least six large studies of the effects of early supplementary feeding on human development were implemented in different parts of the world, including the Guatemala study. Although supplementary feeding provided an alternative, and improved, research design to correlational studies, there are important limitations and considerations inherent in quasi-experimental designs as well. Specific issues relating to this study are discussed more fully in Chapter IV.

Developmental Psychobiology and the Effects of PEM on Cognition

Concerns with the putative effects of PEM on cognition that were prevalent in the 1960s were reinforced by innovative thinking in developmental psychobiology. Influential theoreticians postulated that the nature of early experiences resulted in permanent changes in the organization of neural cells in the cerebrum (Hebb, 1949; Hunt, 1961). Experimental research showed that brain parameters and constituents, such as brain weight, neuronal density, and nucleic acid, could be affected by the nature of the interactions that the organism had with its environment (Rosenzweig, 1966).

Similarly, the notion of critical periods in development was a compelling argument advanced in the late 1960s in support of a paradigm that related particular early experiences with later behavioral attributes. During its early development, the central nervous system was considered particularly vulnerable to teratogenic agents or to particular social stimuli (Bronfenbrenner, 1968; Scott, 1962). This line of thinking provided further justification for the hypothesis that early PEM results in permanent developmental changes (Pryor, 1974)—its face validity was obvious.

Research conducted during this period on the effects of early experience on development generally fit the main effect model and, in particular, the traditional biomedical model of disease causation, namely, that a given pathogen will lead to a specific disease. There was little regard for social and environmental factors as modifiers of the potential effects of early biological trauma; study designs focused on a linear cause-and-effect relation. The agent would be defined as "cultural" or "environmental deprivation," while the effect ("disease") was a comparatively low score on a mental test such as the Stanford-Binet. There were also attempts to define the mechanisms through which "deprivation" worked (Bernstein, 1961; Hess & Shipman, 1965, 1967).

Within this line of thinking, it seemed an urgent necessity to develop technologies to prevent or remediate the adverse effects of an impoverished environment through early intervention programs (Consortium for Longitudinal Studies, 1983). It also made sense that the War on Poverty would be launched and that it should include programs such as Head Start to prevent or remediate the effects of poverty and malnutrition. Work on the effects of early educational interventions on behavioral development was compatible with the notion that early supplementary feeding could prevent the emergence of effects of malnutrition among children living in severe poverty. The hypotheses formulated in both lines of endeavor were similar, and they called for a reductionistic approach that fit the biomedical model. This was attractive to many researchers, particularly in nutrition, where laboratory research and animal models were the preferred form of investigation.

In sum, theory and research in international nutrition and in developmental psychobiology during the 1960s provided strong justification for major experimental studies of PEM and its effects on mental development. Assumptions made at that time regarding the epidemiology of PEM, and the proposition that early experience during critical periods of brain growth could have lasting effects, provided strong support for the notion that protein was a major limiting nutritional factor among undernourished children and that PEM was a major biological trauma. Similarly, recognition of the limitations of observational studies conducted on humans and of experiments with laboratory animals supported the adoption of experimental designs that included early supplementary feeding as the key independent variable.

In the 1960s, the Institute of Nutrition of Central America and Panama (INCAP) was already a leading international nutrition institution. This experience of the institute's staff in field studies and the institute's attractiveness to prestigious scientists in nutrition epidemiology made it natural for INCAP to take a leadership role in this area of research by launching a quasi-experimental study that was intended to yield unique information on the effects of early nutrition on cognitive development.

The research design of the Guatemala study has included a period of longitudinal study spanning the years 1969–1977 and a cross-sectional follow-up during part of 1988–1989. In the next chapter, we describe the villages and the subjects chosen as well as the methods and results of the longitudinal study. Chapter III provides the conceptual underpinnings for the 1988 follow-up, including a review of the relevant literature as well as a discussion of how knowledge gained in the years since the inception of the Guatemala study might have led to a different conceptual and methodological approach. Chapter IV discusses the assumptions and deficiencies inherent in the original design that imposed limitations in the 1988

5

follow-up. Chapters V, VI, and VII present the methods and the results of the follow-up and a discussion of its findings. Chapter VII also presents what we believe to be the mechanisms underlying the observed relations between nutritional input and behavioral changes and the policy implications of these data. One of our main concerns is with the way in which the results that we obtained may be used in justifying nutrition intervention studies among nutritionally at-risk children.

II. METHODOLOGY AND FINDINGS OF THE LONGITUDINAL STUDY

The Guatemala study was designed as a clinical prospective trial in which subjects were exposed to either a high-calorie, high-protein supplement (Atole) or a low-calorie supplement (Fresco). Medical care was made available to both groups. As noted earlier, data collection included longitudinal and cross-sectional follow-up components. This chapter focuses on the former and presents the methods used for developmental assessments conducted in infancy and the preschool years, a review of published findings, and the results of a recent reanalysis of data from these two early developmental periods.

THE VILLAGES

Selection Criteria

The criteria (adapted from Division of Human Development, 1977) used for initial selection of villages included population size (between 500 and 1,000 inhabitants), social isolation (distance from Guatemala City of 35–150 km),[3] educational level (30% literacy among the population aged 8 years and over), and high prevalence of PEM (protein energy malnutrition) as well as gastrointestinal and respiratory infections. All villages were 100% Ladino (i.e., Spanish speaking, not Indian), and each was clustered in a compact, nuclear settlement, with low population mobility (80% or more born in the vicinity) and little likelihood of immediate change.

Of the 300 villages that were investigated, 179 proved eligible on the basis of distance from Guatemala City, ethnicity, and number of inhabitants. When communities without roads and with dispersed settlements were elim-

---

[3] The nearest community included in the study was more than 10 km from Guatemala City and in a different municipality.

inated, the number dropped to 45. A population census conducted in 16 of these 45 communities showed that 10 fell within the predetermined limits.

In all 10 villages, anthropometric, morbidity, and dietary information was collected and the heights and weights of all children aged 5–7 years obtained. On the basis of the comparability of this information, two pairs of villages—one of the pair large (approximately 900 inhabitants per village) and the other small (approximately 500 inhabitants per village)—were selected. Within each pair, assignment of a village to Atole or to Fresco supplementation was random.

Description of the Villages

The villages are located in the Department of El Progreso, a dry, mountainous area northeast of Guatemala City. The distance between each village and Guatemala City ranges from 36 to 102 km; the latitude is around 14°50', and the elevation ranges from 275 to 1,250 m above sea level. The prevailing temperatures range from about 14° to 32° C, with the rainy season occurring from June to October. The two major crops in each village are corn and beans; tomatoes, sorghum, and yuca are also important.

In 1967, less than 10% of the families in the four villages had any source of water at their homes. Almost everyone obtained water from open, hand-dug wells, except in one village, where it was obtained from a nearby river. There was no grey water drainage system in any of the villages, and there were virtually no households with a latrine or any other formal means of feces disposal.

In three of the four villages, the typical house had one to two rooms with adobe walls, dirt floors, and a tile or metal roof. In the remaining village, where the climate is warmest, most houses had thatched roofs, walls made of reeds and mud, and dirt floors. Families usually prepared food either in a separate room or in a separate area located just outside the house. Most people owned their homes as well as at least some of the surrounding land.

About one-third of the families had radios; only a few (fewer than 5%) owned a television, record player, refrigerator, or bicycle. No homes were equipped with electricity.

The primary source of income for most villagers was agricultural production. Almost all villagers were tenant farmers or small landowners; no one reported being a large landholder, and very few reported being merchants. Very few women reported having occupations outside the household, except in one village, where women earned money independently through basket weaving.

In general, parents' literacy levels were low. The proportion of mothers who reported being at least partially literate ranged from 25% to 40% across villages; literacy levels of the fathers were slightly higher, ranging from 38% to 60%.

The pool of potential subjects included all children aged 7 years or younger who lived in the villages at the time the study was initiated, all children who moved into the villages during the course of the project, and all children who were born in the villages between January 1, 1969, and February 28, 1977. All children residing in the village at the time designated for their assessment (at ages 6, 15, and 24 months for the Composite Infant Scale and on the birthdays of children aged 3–7 years for the preschool battery) were eligible for testing. In all, 2,393 children are included in the data set, although the number of subjects for whom data are available on any given variable is considerably lower. Sample sizes at each age for the tests of mental development ranged from 469 at 6 months to 857 at 4 years. These numbers represent coverage rates of 90% or above of potential age-eligible children present in the villages at the time of testing (Division of Human Development, n.d.).

EXPERIMENTAL INTERVENTION

Two villages (one from each pair) were provided with Atole and the other two with Fresco. Since at the time the longitudinal study began it was assumed that the amount of calories contained in Fresco was insufficient to have a developmental effect, it was administered as a placebo.

The Atole supplement was a warm, thick, brown, sweet drink, similar to the corn gruels that Guatemalan mothers often give their children. It was based on a food supplement, Incaparina, developed at INCAP to serve as a high-protein substitute for the traditional corn drink, mixed with dry skim milk and sugar. The Atole contained 11.5 g of protein per cup (180 ml) and 163 kcal of energy per cup.

The control drink, Fresco, was a cool, clear, sweet drink (like KoolAid) and was also common in these villages. At 59 kcal per cup, it contained approximately one-third the calories of Atole and no protein. Both Atole and Fresco were fortified with vitamins and minerals (for their specific composition, see Table 1).

The supplement was available twice daily (10 A.M. and 2 P.M.), seven days a week, in a central feeding station that was located in each village next to the central plaza. Each person who entered the center was given a cup of supplement (180 ml), and the name of the recipient was noted. If requested, infants were given the supplement in a bottle. People sat at one of the five to six round tables in the room to drink their supplement; those who wanted it were given more. When the subject had finished, the cup

TABLE 1

FORMULAS AND NUTRIENT CONTENTS OF ATOLE AND FRESCO

	Atole	Fresco		Atole	Fresco
Ingredients (g/180 ml):			Nutrients (per 180 ml):		
Incaparina[a]	13.5	...	Ascorbic acid (mg) ...	4.0	4.0
Dry skim milk	21.5	...	Calcium (g)	.4	...
Sugar	9.0	13.3	Phosphorus (g)	.3	...
Flavoring agent	...	2.1	Thiamine (mg)	1.1	1.1
Nutrients (per 180 ml):			Riboflavin (mg)	1.5	1.5
Energy (kcal)	163.0	59.0	Niacin (mg)	13.5	13.5
Protein (g)	11.5	...	Vitamin A (mg)	1.2	1.2
Fats (g)	.7	...	Iron (mg)	5.4	5.0
Carbohydrates (g) ...	27.8	15.3	Fluoride (mg)	.2	.2

NOTE.—Both preparations were distributed daily from January 1, 1969, to February 28, 1977. Vitamins and minerals were added to the Fresco on October 1, 1971.

[a] Incaparina is a vegetable protein mixture developed by INCAP. It is marketed in Central America by private industry.

was turned in, and the amount left over was recorded to 10 ml. The supplement was available to every resident of the village, but ingestion was recorded only for target subjects, namely, pregnant and lactating women aged 15 years and older and children up to age 7. Children tended to come with their mothers until the age of 3 or 4; after that, they usually came with older siblings. As they got older, they came by themselves or with their younger siblings.

EFFECTS OF EXPERIMENTAL INTERVENTION ON INFANT AND PRESCHOOL DEVELOPMENT

During the longitudinal study, the behavioral development of the participating children was assessed during the infancy and preschool periods. This section describes the methods and the results that have already been published on the basis of data obtained from these assessments.

Infancy

Measurement

The Brazelton Neonatal Assessment (Brazelton, 1973) was administered to infants born into the study within the first 28 days of life. Its purpose is to assess infant responsiveness, motor organization, and modulation of state. Infants born into the study between 1970 and 1974 were visited in their homes for purposes of administration. Infants born after 1974 were not assessed since they would not be age eligible for preschool battery testing prior to the termination of the study.

A Composite Infant Scale (administered later in infancy) was designed to assess mental and motor development in a culturally appropriate manner. The test was constructed from items drawn from the Bayley, Gesell, Psyche Cattell, and Merrill-Palmer infant scales and from the Stanford-Binet IQ test and adapted for Guatemalan populations on samples in Guatemala City. Assignment of items to the mental or motor category was based on Bayley's (1969) classification (Lasky, Klein, Yarbrough, & Kallio, 1981).

The Composite Infant Scale (CIS) scores represented the sum of mental or motor items passed at each age level. The maximum number of items was 94 at 6 months, 61 at 15 months, and 59 at 24 months. Details of this scale's construction and refinement can be found in Lasky, Klein, Yarbrough, Engle, et al. (1981) and Lasky, Klein, Yarbrough, and Kallio (1981).

Procedure

The test was administered at 6, 15, and 24 months (± 2 weeks). Testing occurred in homelike adobe rooms adjacent to the feeding center, with the mother or an adult caregiver present. For the 6- and 15-month tests, the child was seated on the mother's lap.

The four psychometrists were Guatemalan primary school teachers who received 2 months of training before administering the battery. In addition, standardization sessions—aimed at ensuring that all four testers followed identical procedures—were held every 6 months in day-care centers in Guatemala City. Testers were rotated between the villages given Fresco or between those given Atole.

Data on interobserver reliabilities, test-retest stability, and intercorrelations between mental and motor scores have been reported elsewhere (Lasky, Klein, Yarbrough, & Kallio, 1981). Interobserver reliabilities were high (ranging between .80 and .90), as were test-retest reliability coefficients (ranging between .78 and .91), with one exception—motor scale at 24 months ($r = .48$).

Review of Published Findings

The studies that we review here are restricted to those that have been published and whose specific focus was to test the effects of supplementation on developmental outcomes. Of the only two infant studies that met these criteria, one reported the effects of maternal supplementation on the Brazelton Neonatal Assessment Scale (Brazelton, Tronick, Lechtig, Lasky, & Klein, 1977). Items on the Brazelton Scales were clustered into four groups, with categories 1 and 2 suggesting well-organized behavior and categories 3 and 4 indicative of poor central nervous system functioning. Subjects were divided into quartiles on the basis of mothers' caloric ingestion. Analysis of variance (mothers' supplementation × Neonatal Assessment Scale cluster) failed to establish any statistically significant associations between extent of supplementation of the mothers and neonatal performance.

In the other study (Klein, Arenales, et al., 1976), infants from Atole and Fresco villages were combined and categorized into three groups according to the level of supplemental calories (high, medium, or low) ingested by both the mother and the infant up to the age of testing. The high-intake group was defined by consumption of 10,000 kcal or more per quarter for 14 quarters, the medium-intake group by consumption of from 5,000 to 9,999 kcal, and the low-intake group by consumption of fewer than 5,000 kcal.

Small, albeit statistically significant, differences ($p < .05$) in the Composite Infant Scale mental development scores of the three subgroups were obtained at all three ages tested (6, 15, and 24 months), with greater consumption being associated with a higher score. At 6, 15, and 24 months, the differences between the highest- and lowest-calorie-intake subgroups were 4.0, 9.4, and 6.5 points, respectively. Between-subgroup differences at the same ages on the motor scale were 3.0, 8.8, and 11.4, reaching statistical significance at 15 and 24 months. In all instances, the highest and lowest scores were obtained in the groups with the highest and lowest calorie intake, respectively.

Preschool Years

Measures

The preschool battery consisted of 10 tests administered annually to all children aged 3–7 years and an additional set of 12 tests administered annually to all children aged 5–7 years (10 of this total of 22 tests were introduced in 1971 to assess cognitive domains that had not previously been included). The battery was designed to test traditional indices of cognitive development (e.g., embedded figures, verbal inferences) as well as Piagetian concepts (e.g., conservation).

Test-retest stability coefficients were calculated in three separate studies (conducted in 1969, 1971, and 1974), with a 1-month interval (on average) between test and retest. With about 20 subjects per age and gender in each study, a broad range of stability coefficients was obtained between tests (.0–.95) as well as within tests (at different assessments; e.g., .09–.81). A complete list of reliability coefficients for each test is reported in Appendix A.

Interobserver reliability was calculated every 6 months, at the time testers standardized their testing procedures. In this standardization, one tester administered the instrument, and the other three simultaneously recorded the child's responses. Mean interobserver reliability was .95 or above on all tests (Townsend et al., 1982).

The validity of the battery was established through correlations with village adults' judgments of the "brightness" of particular children (Klein, Freeman, Spring, Nerlove, & Yarbrough, 1976). The test battery was also found to correlate with children's behavior, specifically, with their ability to carry out complex sequences of behavior (chores) (Nerlove, Roberts, Klein, Yarbrough, & Habicht, 1974). In addition, test performance was associated with age of entry into school and with school achievement (Gorman & Pollitt, 1993; Irwin, Engle, Yarbrough, Klein, & Townsend, 1978) as well as with measures of stimulation provided by parents at home, SES, and house quality (Freeman, Klein, Townsend, & Lechtig, 1980).

Procedure

Testing occurred within 1 month of the child's birthday. As with the infant battery, the testing took place in adobe huts adjacent to the supplementation centers. Given the number of tests, testing of 3- and 4-year-olds took two sessions and that of 5–7-year-olds three sessions on three different days. As with the infant battery, the testers were Guatemalan primary school teachers who had received extensive training and who were submitted to frequent standardization.

Review of Published Findings

The three published studies of the effects of the treatment on measures of preschool cognitive abilities (Engle, Yarbrough, & Klein, 1983; Freeman et al., 1980; Townsend et al., 1982) have reported small but statistically significant relations between treatment and outcomes. Two of these studies (Engle et al., 1983; Freeman et al., 1980) employed designs other than the original Atole-Fresco comparison: subjects were pooled, and energy consumption (e.g., calories) was used as the treatment variable. The strength of the experimental design was thereby lost, and this change in analytic strategy negated the possibility of testing the original between-group hypothesis.

The samples of these three studies varied with respect to the degree of exposure to the supplementation, and the outcome variables selected for analyses differed. Freeman et al. (1980) focused on only a few measures, whereas Townsend et al. (1982) reported on almost all the tests included in the battery. In some cases, a "cognitive composite" score—an unweighted standardized average of selected tests—was constructed and used for analysis (Engle et al., 1983; Townsend et al., 1982).

At most ages, comparisons of test scores obtained in Fresco and Atole small and large villages favored Atole children (Townsend et al., 1982); this held for 22% of the comparisons in the large villages and 29% in the small ones. Positive associations were obtained between supplement consumption and performance on tests of language, memory, and perception (Freeman et al., 1980) as well as on two different composite scores (Engle et al., 1983; Freeman et al., 1980). In one of these studies, the effects were observed primarily in boys (Engle et al., 1983), whereas, in another, they were restricted to girls (Townsend et al., 1982).

Effects of treatment on social-emotional behavior were reported in the fourth published study (Barrett, Radke-Yarrow, & Klein, 1983). After the intervention had been terminated, subjects from three of the villages were assessed on measures of social interaction and affect. The subjects were pooled across treatment groups and classified as high, medium, or low consumers on the basis of both the mother's ingestion during pregnancy and the child's supplementation up to 4 years of age. High supplementation was found to be associated with higher levels of social involvement and affect (both positive and negative), whereas low levels of supplementation were associated with passivity, dependency, and anxious behavior (Barrett et al., 1983). Although these findings are in the hypothesized direction, the absence of a between-group analysis raises questions about their interpretation. Pooling subjects and using amount of calories ingested as the treatment variable make the possibility of a self-selection bias quite plausible since mothers and infants with the highest levels of consumption may in fact also have been the most socially engaged among the subjects.

The fact that these four studies differed in design, sample, and outcome variables accounts for the variation in reported findings and also poses difficulties for their interpretation. Nonetheless, the results do converge in showing small yet fairly consistent effects of the Atole supplementation.

To obtain a clearer understanding of the data, we reanalyzed the infant and preschool data following the original design. In the remaining portion of this chapter, we describe the methodology of the reanalyses and provide a summary of the findings.

METHODS OF THE CURRENT ANALYSES

Infancy

Data from the Composite Infant Scale were analyzed using the mental and motor scores obtained at each of the three ages: 6, 15, and 24 months. In contrast to previously published studies, the new analyses were restricted to an Atole/Fresco comparison of a cohort of subjects who were exposed to the treatment both pre- and postnatally. A general linear model was used to analyze the data, with treatment entered as a class variable. All analyses controlled for socioeconomic status (SES), sex, and attendance and included a treatment × SES interactive term (a complete description of the socioeconomic and attendance variables is given in Chaps. V and VI, respectively).

Preschool

To reduce the large numbers of tests included in the preschool battery, the battery was factor analyzed (with varimax rotation) before undertaking the current analyses. Only tests considered to have minimally acceptable test-retest stability coefficients (.6 or above for most age/sex groups) were included in this analysis. Several other tests were also eliminated from consideration because the scoring system was ambiguous (i.e., Reversal Discrimination Learning Test II), because the data file was unavailable (i.e., Animal House), or because the tests did not load with any other measures in exploratory factor analyses (Conservation of Matter, Incidental and Intentional Learning). Finally, two tests—Verbal Inferences and Knox Cubes—were not included at age 3 owing to very high rates of missing data. All tests that were used for the factor analysis are listed in Appendix B.

The results of this analysis are presented in Table 2. At all ages, the first factor accounted for about 35% of the variance and the second for between 22% and 9%, declining with the age of the children. A third factor, with eigenvalues below 1 at all ages, was dropped from further analyses.

The first factor represents a general perceptual-organizational (Embedded Figures Test, Incomplete Figures, Odd Figures, Block Design, and Memory for Designs) and a verbal (Verbal Analogies, Memory for Objects, and Vocabulary Recognition) factor. The second loads most heavily on digit and sentence memory at all ages. The two other tests labeled as memory

15

TABLE 2

FACTOR LOADING FROM VARIMAX ROTATION FOR PRESCHOOL BATTERY TESTS

	AGE IN YEARS				
TEST	3	4	5	6	7
General factor (Factor 1):					
Embedded Figures	.78	.40	.14	.58	.59
Digit Memory	.06	.04	.04	.05	.17
Sentence Memory	.28	.37	.26	.23	.22
Recognition Vocabulary	.81	.72	.58	.54	.69
Draw-a-Line	−.22	−.10	−.53	−.32	−.46
Puzzle	−.09	−.03	.00	.09	.16
Memory for Objects	.63	.71	.42	.19	.53
Verbal Inferences		.61	.37	.52	.57
Knox Cubes: Slow			.62	.61	.35
Incomplete Figures			.62	.70	.74
Odd Figure			.47	.69	.74
Block Design			.60	.69	.58
Memory for Designs			.57	.72	.69
Eigenvalues	1.81	1.72	2.71	3.18	3.78
Memory factor (Factor 2):					
Embedded Figures	.02	−.03	.09	.10	.13
Digit Memory	.87	.87	.87	.81	.83
Sentence Memory	.81	.74	.82	.79	.85
Recognition Vocabulary	.17	.17	.24	.44	.17
Draw-a-Line	−.08	−.46	−.27	−.45	−.28
Puzzle	.13	.00	.05	.09	.01
Memory for Objects	.24	.05	.24	.45	.05
Verbal Inferences		.28	.41	.45	.11
Knox Cubes: Slow			.00	.19	−.28
Incomplete Figures			.17	.37	.15
Odd Figure			.11	.16	.11
Block Design			.03	.16	.15
Memory for Designs			−.03	.23	.07
Eigenvalues	1.52	1.64	1.85	2.73	1.73

NOTE.—Sample size is over 600 per age group.

measures (Memory for Objects and Memory for Designs) loaded primarily on the first factor, suggesting that these assess cognitive skills other than the verbal repetition required in the Memory for Sentences and Digit Memory tests. The Draw-a-Line Slowly test loaded on both factors.

Cross-age correlations within each factor suggest moderate stability ranging between .29 and .67 for Factor 1 and between .26 and .66 for Factor 2. In general, the magnitude of these coefficients increased with age.

As with the Composite Infant Scale, analyses were restricted to an Atole-Fresco comparison of a cohort of subjects who had been exposed to the treatment both pre- and postnatally. At least 100 subjects were available at ages 3, 4, 5, and 6 years, but their number was too small ($N = 13$) to

TABLE 3

Results of Regression (General Linear Model) of Composite Infant Scores on Treatment for Maximum Exposure Cohort

Variable Name	N	R^2	Treatment[a]
6 months:			
Mental	279	.02	−.007
Motor	279	.03	−.035
15 months:			
Mental	274	.03	1.12†
Motor	274	.03	1.59†
24 months:			
Mental	242	.05*	.157
Motor	242	.12***	4.58***

[a] The value reflects the least square mean difference (Atole − Fresco), adjusted for SES (house quality, father's occupation, mother's schooling), sex, and attendance.
† $p < .10$.
* $p < .05$.
*** $p < .001$.

permit analysis of the 7-year data. In addition to age-specific scores, two composite factor scores were calculated by summing across ages for individuals with data at multiple time points. All these data were analyzed using general linear model regression and entering treatment as a class variable. Analyses adjusted for sex, attendance, and SES and included a treatment × SES interactive term.

TABLE 4

Results of Regression (General Linear Model) of Treatment on Preschool Battery Scores

Variable Name	N	R^2	Treatment[a]
3 years:			
Factor 1	260	.05*	.090
Factor 2	260	.04	.176
4 years:			
Factor 1	248	.06*	.269*
Factor 2	248	.01	.064
5 years:			
Factor 1	178	.07†	.489**
Factor 2	178	.04	−.221
6 years:			
Factor 1	101	.09	.152
Factor 2	101	.09	−.289

[a] The value reflects the least square mean difference (Atole − Fresco), adjusted for SES (house quality, father's occupation, mother's schooling), sex, and attendance.
† $p < .10$.
* $p < .05$.
** $p < .01$.

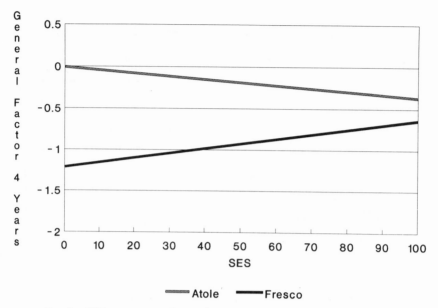

FIG. 1.—SES × treatment interaction: General factor score at age 4 years

RESULTS OF THE CURRENT ANALYSES

Composite Infant Scale.—Of the six new analyses of the infant data, only one showed an effect of treatment: Atole children had significantly higher scores on the motor scale at 24 months than Fresco subjects (see Table 3). When interactive terms were entered into the model, no significant interactions of treatment with either a composite SES variable or sex emerged.

Preschool battery.—After adjusting for all other covariates in the model (sex, attendance, and SES), a main effect of treatment was obtained at 4 and 5 years on Factor 1 scores, with Atole subjects performing significantly better than Fresco subjects (see Table 4). No differences between treatment groups on Factor 2 scores were obtained at any age.

There was a significant main effect of gender at age 4 years, with girls scoring higher than boys on the verbal factor score. When the treatment × SES interactive term was entered into the model, significant interactions at 4 and 5 years emerged on the first factor. At both these ages, SES was not associated with performance in the Atole subjects, but it was positively related to outcomes in the Fresco villages. As depicted in Figures 1 and 2, the largest differences between treatments were observed in subjects at the lowest end of the socioeconomic distribution; as SES improved, differences between groups were less evident.

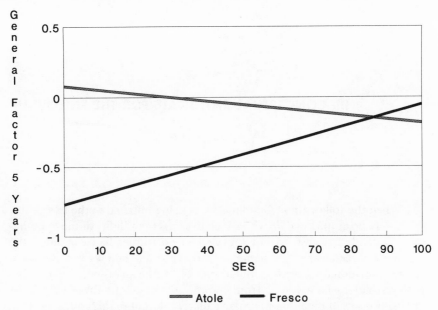

FIG. 2.—SES × treatment interaction: General factor score at age 5 years

CONCLUSIONS

We tested the hypothesis that the provision of protein-calorie supplementation prenatally and during the first 2 years of a child's life would have an effect on cognitive functioning during the infant and preschool years. The test of the hypothesis was performed using statistical and design controls to increase the internal validity of the conclusions.

The results of previous analyses as well as the reanalyses presented here indicate that there were a few moderately beneficial effects from exposure to the Atole supplement. These effects were strongest in children from the neediest families (as determined by an SES composite score). Issues regarding differences in the reported effects as a function of age are discussed in Chapter VII. Problems inherent in the original design of the longitudinal study and the methodological difficulties of conducting the follow-up are discussed in other chapters.

III. CONCEPTUAL RATIONALE FOR THE FOLLOW-UP

When the follow-up in Guatemala was being initiated in the late 1980s, there were no empirical data with which to assess the validity of the hypothesis we intended to test: to our knowledge, no studies had examined the relation between early supplementary feeding and adolescent cognition among nutritionally at-risk populations. Thus, the plausibility of our hypothesis had to be assessed from indirect evidence. In this chapter, we discuss two sets of data that were particularly relevant to this endeavor. One of these consists of studies that examined the effects of early supplementary feeding on mental development in early childhood and the other of evaluations of long-term effects of compensatory early childhood educational interventions on adolescent development.

The issue of plausibility also had to take account of contemporary views in developmental psychology and nutrition. Since the inception of the Guatemala longitudinal study in 1969, major changes had taken place in theories of human development. One critical change had been a move away from a main effect (biomedical) model of developmental risk. In contrast to views prevailing in the 1960s, it is currently recognized that, in general, exposure to a single risk factor in early childhood does not necessarily determine a developmental course; rather, the effects of exposure are often viewed as modified by multiple factors both in and outside the child. As such, contemporary views have increased the complexity of explanatory models and called into doubt the possibility that successful strategies for developmental intervention can be restricted to monofocal interventions.

DEVELOPMENTAL EFFECTS OF EARLY NUTRITION INTERVENTIONS

As noted in the previous chapter, the published reports of the longitudinal study differed in the criteria used to select samples, in the cognitive tests chosen for analyses, and in the definition of the treatment variable.

Thus, only tentative inferences concerning the effects of the nutritional intervention on behavioral development were justified.

However, additional support for these inferences emerged from three other major intervention studies (of more than 100 subjects) that were launched at about the same time as the Guatemala study. One of these was conducted in Bogota, Colombia (Lutter et al., 1989; Super, Herrera, & Mora, 1991; Waber et al., 1981), the second in Sui Lin, Taiwan (Adair & Pollitt, 1985; Joos, Pollitt, Mueller, & Albright, 1983), and the third in New York City (Rush, Stein, & Susser, 1980). All these investigations tested the proposition that PEM (protein energy malnutrition) limited cognitive development in childhood. However, despite similar objectives, they differed widely in research designs, criteria for sample selection, nutritional status of the subjects, type and timing of supplementation, and behavioral outcomes selected for study (Pollitt & Oh, 1992).

Infancy

Published findings from these intervention studies are restricted to the infancy period. In two of these, early supplementary feeding had positive effects on the mental (Waber et al., 1981) and the motor (Joos et al., 1983; Waber et al., 1981) development of infants. Infants exposed to a nutritional supplement during gestation and the first years of postnatal life performed better than control subjects on mental and motor development scales; the sizes of the effects were equivalent to about .20 of a standard deviation. In the third study, no effects were reported (Rush et al., 1980).

Since the 1987 follow-up in Guatemala was begun, two additional reports on the effects of a high-calorie supplement on infant development have also been published. One study was conducted in Kingston, Jamaica (Grantham-McGregor, Powell, Walker, & Himes, 1991), and the other in West Java, Indonesia (Husaini, Karyadi, Husaini, Sandjaja, Karyadi, & Pollitt, 1991). Their findings agreed in part with the previous studies in showing that nutritional intervention had beneficial effects on the motor, but not on the mental, development of infants and young children.

To further test the proposition that, in nutritionally at-risk populations, early supplementary feeding is sufficient to improve infant development, the five studies noted above and the data from Guatemala were pooled in a meta-analysis. This analysis was restricted to comparisons between experimental groups exposed solely to a nutritional supplement and controls. The samples were stratified by age: one group included infants aged from 8 to 15 months and the other those aged from 18 to 24 months.

The results of the meta-analysis showed a significant effect of supplementation on motor development scores in both age groups ($p < .01$), but significant effects on mental test scores were limited to the older group of infants (Pollitt & Oh, 1992). These data strengthen the hypothesis that early nutritional intervention has an effect on cognitive development, at least during the first 2 years of life.

Preschool Period

Results beyond the infancy period were available from two studies. IQ data obtained at age 5 years from the Taiwan study were published by Hsueh and Meyer (1981); the children were no longer being supplemented at that time since the intervention had ceased with weaning. In contrast to the infancy findings, the supplementation was not associated with IQ. Data on preschoolers from the Bogota study have also recently become available (Super et al., 1991). Three and a half years after the end of the intervention (mean age = 6.74 years), the children were assessed on an achievement test containing items of reading readiness, arithmetic, and basic knowledge. Significant effects accounting for about 8 months of cognitive growth were observed in reading readiness; these effects were more likely to be found in families in which mothers had substantial psychological and social resources.

Although studies of the consequences of early supplementary feeding on the development of infants and preschool-aged children are not directly relevant to the plausibility of the hypothesis of long-term effects, they did provide some backing for our contention. Taken together, their results showed that nutritional intervention was sufficient to affect early behavioral development among nutritionally at-risk infants and preschoolers.

LONG-TERM EFFECTS OF EARLY EDUCATIONAL INTERVENTIONS

Data on the developmental consequences of early educational interventions for children raised in poverty were relevant to the hypothesis of the follow-up for at least two reasons. First, the nutritional and the educational intervention studies shared similar theoretical views concerning developmental continuity, and, second, the latter offered a unique opportunity to examine the effects of early experience on adolescent outcomes.

The genesis of the early education programs in the United States was related to the claims made in the 1960s that the prevalence of poverty and malnutrition in the United States was much higher than had been thought. This concern was intensified when behavioral scientists recognized that the cognitive and socioemotional development of children was at risk after exposure to such conditions. One response to this concern was the creation of Head Start, which had as its primary objective the prevention of adverse developmental effects associated with life in poverty.

Important theoretical similarities exist between the attempts to foster mental development through early supplementary feeding and through preschool educational interventions. The contention was that exposure to risk factors such as malnutrition and poor home environment would in part determine the course of human development. However, it was also assumed that the developmental deficits associated with poverty could be prevented by such social and political programs as WIC (Women, Infants, and Children) and Head Start. In line with these views of developmental continuity was the notion of critical periods; the concern among behavioral scientists was that changing the course of an individual's development would be more difficult after it had been set by adverse early experiences.

Among the early intervention programs begun during this period, some of the most influential have been the 11 studies conducted by the Consortium for Longitudinal Studies (1983). These preschool cognitively oriented interventions led to moderate IQ gains in early childhood, at the time when the children were about to enroll in kindergarten. However, evaluations conducted 2–3 years later yielded disappointing results. The IQ gains that had been observed had either declined or disappeared, so the benefits seemed to have been short lived (Bronfenbrenner, 1974, 1979). Given these results, the findings of a subsequent follow-up (conducted in 1975) were surprising: although the previously reported decline in IQ was maintained, new benefits emerged. Assessments of grade retention in school, special education placement, school attendance, health, juvenile delinquency rates, and adolescent pregnancies showed that the experimental subjects fared better than the controls.

The data generated by these early education programs provided additional indirect support for the hypothesis we intended to test. Taken together with the data on early nutritional intervention, they provided strong support for the contention that the hypothesis we proposed did merit testing.

SUPPLEMENTARY FEEDING AND CURRENT VIEWS ON DEVELOPMENT

As noted earlier, the plausibility of the hypothesis we proposed required considering whether the data to be obtained could be interpreted in light of contemporary views on human development and nutrition. A related issue was whether data required to explain any findings in contemporary terms existed since data collection during the previous intervention period had been limited. These concerns were accentuated by the long interval between the experiment and the follow-up.

Many assumptions that dominated developmental psychology in the

1960s—such as the unique importance of infancy, developmental continuity, and the effects of exposure to early biological risk factors—have been challenged in the last 20 years. It is now accepted that, albeit with exceptions, the nature and intensity of a trauma in early life are not the single determinants of developmental risk (Horowitz, 1987; Sameroff & Chandler, 1975). The calculation of risk must take into account both the degree of resiliency (or vulnerability) of the organism and the attributes of the environment in which a child lives (Farran & McKinney, 1986). Accordingly, holding a risk factor constant, the probability of recovery from exposure to such a factor will vary among children (Rutter & Pickles, 1991).

The studies conducted by Werner and Smith (1977, 1982, 1992; see also Werner, Bierman, & French, 1971) provide a clear illustration of the power of the interaction between person and environment. These investigators followed a cohort born in 1955 in Kauai from infancy to adulthood; the aim was to estimate the predictive value of biological and social stresses experienced during the perinatal and infant periods. Their most recent publication (Werner & Smith, 1992) reports that the long-term consequences of most biological risk conditions depend on the quality of the rearing environment: if a child was raised in a supportive and rewarding family environment, the probability of developmental deviance faded, independent of the nature of the risk factor.

Similar differences between past and present conceptualizations exist in the area of developmental nutrition. As noted in Chapter I, in the 1960s, inadequate provision of protein in the diets of infants and young children in low-income groups in the less developed countries was viewed as the limiting factor. This notion was a catalyst for the conceptualization and research design of the Guatemala study. Since then, it has been recognized that energy and micronutrients also play critical roles in human development. Mild to moderate deficiencies of iodine, iron, zinc, and vitamin A, for example, have functional effects that can affect development directly or indirectly (Levin, Pollitt, Galloway, & McGuire, in press).

From the outset, we recognized that the original study design would not permit us to carry out a risk analysis that follows contemporary views of human development and nutrition. For instance, as discussed in the next chapter, the data available on supplement consumption and on home dietary intake were not sufficient to determine the possible distinct roles of protein, energy, and micronutrients. Similarly, the data on the subjects' social and economic background were restricted to graduated parameters of social structure (e.g., maternal education, father's occupation). There was not enough information on family process variables to estimate the extent to which these modify the effects of the early nutritional supplementation. A similar limitation was the absence of information on the children's social and emotional development, which would have been invaluable in assessing differential responses to treatment as a function of individual differences.

Those constraints, however, do not necessarily preclude an analysis of effect modifiers. Although the available social and economic data index only broad parameters of social structure (so-called social address measures), they nevertheless provide markers of some aspects of the environment that are known to affect differences in behavioral development (Wachs, 1992). This type of information as well as the variability in the subjects' school experiences allowed us to examine differential responses to the nutrition treatment as a function of the general environmental context.

Moreover, the absence of some potentially useful information was generously compensated for by the data that were available. There was a wealth of longitudinal information on the physical growth and morbidity of the children and on the educational systems in the villages in which the study was conducted. This information allowed us an extended view of the effect of the intervention on the lives of these children. Recognition of the breadth of effects has permitted an understanding of the close interrelations between growth and development as well as an awareness of some of the multiple mechanisms that may mediate the relations between early supplementary feeding and behavioral outcomes.

The next chapter provides a detailed discussion of the limitations inherent in the design of the longitudinal study as well as of those that resulted from conditions of the follow-up. The choice of the analytic strategy that we pursued will derive naturally from a discussion of these issues.

IV. METHODOLOGICAL AND
SUBSTANTIVE CONSIDERATIONS

INHERENT LIMITATIONS OF THE LONGITUDINAL
AND FOLLOW-UP STUDIES

The complexities of conducting an experimental intervention study are well known. Quasi-experimental designs, in particular, have limitations, and the inferences that can be drawn from their findings are severely restricted by the degree to which underlying assumptions have been met. In the case of the Guatemala longitudinal study, its mere duration over 10 years presents difficulties of control. Moreover, knowledge gained during the course of the study resulted in ongoing changes in its design and in the interpretation of accumulating findings.

In addition to the limitations of the original study design, there are several considerations related specifically to the conditions of the follow-up. The intervention was carried out between 1969 and 1977; for all practical purposes, the study teams had no further contact with the villages from the end of that period until 1987, when the follow-up was being planned. Major life changes for which no data were available could have occurred during this 10-year gap. In addition, the fact that the original subjects were now adolescents and young adults presented additional methodological difficulties. This chapter addresses some of the most serious concerns regarding the design of the longitudinal study as well as issues that relate specifically to the follow-up.

Equivalence among Villages

Ideal experimental conditions prevail when the only relevant variable that distinguishes the experimental and the control groups is exposure to treatment. One of the most notorious risks associated with quasi-experimental studies is the nonequivalence of groups at pretest (Campbell & Stanley, 1963). Any nontreatment variable that is correlated with the treat-

ment could explain any of the differences in outcome variables, which cannot then be attributed unequivocally to exposure. Similarly, if the treatment and control groups differ along the outcome variables before exposure, then differences observed after exposure cannot be attributed to the treatment.

One way to avoid such potential differences between treatment and control groups is the randomization of treatment. In the Guatemala study, randomization occurred at the village level: one large and one small village were randomly assigned, respectively, to Atole and Fresco. With four villages and randomization occurring only within pairs, it is very likely that errors were not distributed randomly across villages.

Apart from the randomization, villages were assumed to be equivalent in terms of important variables related to the intervention, and the validity of inferences about the effects of treatment rests on the validity of these assumptions. In the case of the Guatemala study, sociodemographic, behavioral, and nutritional equivalence was necessary to control for the potential confounding effects of these factors. Data establishing the initial equivalence of children in Atole and Fresco villages in terms of height, weight, and home diet have been reported (Martorell, Klein, & Delgado, 1980); however, there are no previous analyses testing whether the sociodemographic or cognitive characteristics of the population were equivalent.

Sociodemographic Characteristics

To ascertain initial equivalence in socioeconomic status, we performed comparisons between villages using a 2 (treatment) $\times$ 2 (size) analysis of variance with unbalanced cells (General Linear Model; SAS, 1988) for the continuous measures and a chi-square analysis of treatment within village size for the categorical variables. Because of the original matching of villages by size and the possibility that socioeconomic characteristics would be in part a function of size, village size was included in these analyses.

The measures used in these analyses were derived from 1967 census data (specifics of their derivation are given in Chap. V) and reflected family background variables believed to have theoretical associations with the developmental outcomes: parents' education and literacy levels, house quality, and father's occupation. Since only 5% of mothers reported being employed outside the home, mother's occupation was not analyzed. These measures were constructed for all residents of each village.

Our analysis showed that, in 1967, fathers in the Atole villages had significantly higher-ranked occupations than those residing in the Fresco villages, $F(1, 508) = 5.61, p < .05$. While Atole fathers were more likely to farm their own land (62% vs. 27% for Atole and Fresco, respectively), fathers in Fresco villages more frequently worked as tenant farmers (50% vs.

27

27% for Fresco and Atole, respectively). In contrast, both mothers and fathers in the Fresco villages were more likely to be literate than those in the Atole villages (34% vs. 26% for mothers, $\chi^2[1] = 3.72$, $p < .05$; 53% vs. 38% for fathers, $\chi^2[1] = 12.49$, $p < .01$). There were no differences in house quality by village type.

In sum, the data indicate that the original assumption of the equivalence of social and economic characteristics between villages was not justified: fathers in the Atole villages had higher occupation levels, while both mothers and fathers in the Fresco villages were more likely to be literate. Village size did not covary in any consistent way with any of the socioeconomic variables and was therefore excluded from all further analyses reported in the *Monograph*.

Cognitive Abilities

Family economic background and parents' education are known to be positively associated with children's cognitive development (Garcia-Coll, 1990; Laosa, 1984; Sigman et al., 1988). Given that the villages were not equivalent in terms of the relevant social and economic parameters, it is reasonable to suspect that these pretreatment between-village differences in SES could have been associated with pretreatment cognitive differences. If this were the case, then such differences could be related to differences in cognitive outcome in the adolescent period.

A substitute for the unavailable pretreatment information concerning cognitive abilities is the psychological test scores of the 5–7-year-old children from the Atole and the Fresco villages that were obtained in 1969, during the first year of the study. In comparison to other cohorts, these children would be less likely to have benefited from the supplement because of their late exposure to it. About 50 children from each pair of villages were compared at each of the three ages on the 12 preschool tests administered during this first study year. No consistent differences were found in favor of either group. Among the 5-year-olds, two tests (Incidental and Intentional Learning) favored Fresco children; at 6 years, there were two differences (Digit Memory and Verbal Inferences) in favor of Atole, and, at 7 years, the one difference (Digit Memory) favored Atole as well.

In sum, although social and economic differences between Atole and Fresco villages did exist, the comparisons of preschool cognitive test performance point to no systematic difference in favor of either group; out of 36 comparisons, 8% favor Atole and 6% Fresco. We conclude, therefore, that pretreatment preschool cognitive differences between Atole and Fresco subjects could not account for any differences observed in the adolescent period.

Changes in the Villages—the 10-Year Hiatus

The lack of contiguity between the time of exposure to the treatment and the time of assessment of the adolescent outcome variables makes it nearly impossible to discard the "history" (Cook & Campbell, 1979) threat to validity since a different rate of social and economic growth from village to village could affect differences in the cognitive growth of residents (Bronfenbrenner, 1979). In the following discussion, we contrast data on different parameters of social and economic growth that occurred between 1967 and 1987.[4]

In two of the villages, the main water source had not changed noticeably over the intervening 20 years, and more than 90% of the families still obtained their water from a public well or spigot. In the other two villages, where over 90% of the families had obtained their water from a river or hand-dug wells in 1967, almost all had access to a public spigot or well by 1987, and about half had homes with piped connections to the water system (see Table 5).

In spite of these improvements in water sources, by 1987 only about 5% of the households in each village were hooked up to a piped network for drainage purposes. Similarly, methods of human waste disposal were still not well developed, with only about half the families having any means of sanitation, such as rudimentary septic tanks or latrines in their homes.

Several of the changes that occurred in house quality are notable. As a result of a major earthquake in 1976, many tile roofs were replaced with sheet metal. Cement floors replaced dirt floors in over one-third of the homes in each village (Table 5). As represented by a factor score, the changes in house quality displayed in Table 6 indicate that overall quality increased over time and at similar rates among the villages, although less improvement was evident in one Atole village. Whereas electricity was unavailable in 1967, by 1987 two-thirds to three-quarters of all families had electricity in their homes. Although no differences in house quality were reported in 1967, by 1987 Fresco villages had significantly higher house factor scores than Atole villages. However, although the number of all household possessions had increased, their availability still remained low in 1987. Only 5%–10% of families owned bicycles, refrigerators, or record players, while 15%–30% owned television sets.

The primary means of income for most villagers continued to be agricultural production, with most heads of households employed as tenant farmers or small landowners (see Table 7). The main change in occupation over the years was that the percentage of men involved in skilled trades

---

[4] Suzan Carmichael was responsible for the data analysis of SES changes in the villages. We gratefully acknowledge her contributions to this chapter.

29

TABLE 5

Characteristics of Homes by Village and Year (%)

	Fresco 03	Atole 06	Fresco 08	Atole 14
Percentage of homes with:				
Some means of disposal of human waste:				
1967	7	8	1	5
1974	15	19	24	12
1987	46	65	54	66
Well in house or hookup to public network:				
1967	0	3	7	0
1974	<1	21	15	<1
1987	7	82	71	9
Nondirt floors:				
1967	5	5	12	2
1974	13	13	16	10
1987	62	27	38	28
Adobe walls:				
1967	59	31	11	71
1974	83	47	20	83
1987	82	73	7	65
Separate kitchens:				
1967	64	40	56	77
1974	87	61	69	87
1987	94	85	82	88

Note.—Villages are identified by census codes.

TABLE 6

Changes in SES Indicators by Village and Year

	Fresco 03	Atole 06	Fresco 08	Atole 14
House factor scores:				
1967	2.08	1.77	1.64	2.15
1974	3.18	2.64	2.39	2.97
1987	4.02	3.52	2.39	3.46
Mothers' literacy (%):				
1967	40	25	26	29
1974	51	37	35	39
1987	63	58	58	63
Fathers' literacy (%):				
1967	47	38	60	38
1974	56	49	67	44
1987	65	66	76	61
Population:				
1967	811	854	549	469
1974	995	1,073	760	672
1987	1,636	1,640	1,120	1,135

Note.—Villages are identified by census codes.

TABLE 7

PRINCIPAL OCCUPATION OF FATHERS (%)

	Fresco 03	Atole 06	Fresco 08	Atole 14
Agricultural wage labor:				
1967	6	3	21	15
1974	5	7	29	4
1987	5	5	38	2
Tenant farmer:				
1967	58	28	42	26
1974	54	33	30	34
1987	29	19	22	28
Small landowner:				
1967	26	68	28	56
1974	27	53	28	55
1987	17	52	15	40
Skilled trade:				
1967	8	<1	7	0
1974	14	7	11	4
1987	47	21	21	28
Merchant:				
1967	1	1	2	2
1974	1	0	2	3
1987	2	2	4	3

NOTE.—Villages are identified by census codes.

had increased from very few in 1967 to 47% in 1987 in one Fresco village and to between 20% and 30% in the other three villages. By 1987, the previous differences between Atole and Fresco in occupation levels among fathers were no longer statistically significant. Women continued infrequently to report having occupations.

Self-reported literacy increased over time at similar rates in all villages, with the same villages maintaining the highest literacy levels. The gap between the literacy rates of women and men was greatly reduced by 1987, except in one Fresco village, where the 76% literacy rate for men was higher than either male or female literacy rates in any of the other villages (see Table 6). The mean level of schooling increased at a much slower rate, with the average years of schooling, like literacy, being higher for men than for women. Differences in parents' literacy rates reported in 1967 continued to be evident, and both mothers' and fathers' levels of education were significantly higher in Fresco than in Atole villages.

Table 6 presents the change from 1967 to 1987 in the total population of each village. Growth rates for the villages appeared similar, with the population in each approximately doubling since 1967. Nuclear family size (mother, father, and offspring living with them) remained fairly stable across the 20-year span (4.6–4.7 in 1967 and 4.6–5.0 in 1987).

In summary, life in the villages had changed, and in many ways improved, over the 20 years since the initial study: electricity and water were more readily available, house quality improved, and illiteracy rates declined. Nonetheless, the change was slow and may not represent substantial reductions in the risks posed to child welfare. For example, although the average number of years of schooling of the adult population in 1987 had approximately doubled since 1967, this change represented an increase of only 1 year of schooling. Similarly, half the families still carried all their water, and in none of the villages was there adequate gray water or sewage disposal.

The history factor cannot be fully discarded in the present study, and anecdotal data suggest that between-village differences in social and economic development may in fact have existed. For instance, the Institute for Cultural Affairs in Guatemala began a large development project in one of the Atole villages shortly after the supplementation study finished in 1977. Bank loans were made available to invest in drip irrigation, running water was installed, and, more recently, a preschool was begun, enabling women to work outside their homes. However, the possibility of between-village differences in social and economic growth must be tempered by the fact that the data collected on social and economic changes in the villages do not point in that direction. There were no marked differences between villages in improvements in water sources, changes in house quality, household possessions, occupation, or parents' education.

Implementation of Treatment

As noted above, an essential element of experimental design is the assumption that the only difference between the experimental and the control groups lies in exposure to treatment. In the case of the Guatemala study, the only difference between groups should have been the nutritional aspects of the intervention. In fact, there were potentially quite important nonnutritional differences between the two treatments: beyond differences in both its real and its perceived nutritional value, Atole differed in name, appearance, and taste.

A second issue relates to the implementation of the intervention. Were there any nonnutritional factors in the delivery of the treatment that might have had effects on the outcomes similar to those expected from the nutritional intervention? Two factors are relevant here: the treatment was not blind, and it was extended to include the mothers.

Because the treatment was not blind, there is a possibility that the field-workers in the Atole and Fresco villages behaved differently toward the respective participants. For instance, field-workers might have given greater encouragement to the mothers to attend the feeding station in the Atole than in the Fresco villages. Consequently, rates of attendance at the feeding stations might have differed between villages. This, in turn, could have resulted in more frequent social interactions between participants and field-workers in the Atole than in the Fresco stations, which could have had a differential effect on the children in the two groups. Although no data are available on interactions between field-workers and subjects or on actual promotion of participation, attendance data are available and will be discussed in a later section.

Distribution of the supplement to the mothers who accompanied the children to the feeding station poses another problem: Atole, but not Fresco, may have had a salutary effect on caretaking behavior, which, in turn, could have fostered cognitive growth in the offspring. This issue, however, cannot be fully addressed because treatment effects on the mothers were not assessed and relevant records (e.g., mothers' weight changes) are restricted to specific periods (i.e., pregnancy and lactation). Hence, it is not possible to test whether treatment effects on mothers occurred and, if so, whether they might act as potential cofounders.

Patterns of Attendance

The original study design assumed that provision of Fresco controlled for the possible confounding effects of attendance and that any differences in outcomes between the Atole and the Fresco subjects could therefore be attributed solely to the nutritional intervention. However, this assumption is valid only if attendance patterns proved to be similar across villages and if the correlates of attendance were also similar in all four sites. We noted earlier that the perception of the benefits of Atole over Fresco and/or selective encouragement by field-workers due to nonblind treatments may have affected participation. Here, we examine data to assess across-village similarities in patterns of attendance and associations between socioeconomic variables and attendance and between attendance and outcome variables.

Attendance rates were computed as the number of times (morning and/ or afternoon) attended per year for each year of the child's life (1–7). A summed composite of the seven individual years was also computed. Atole/ Fresco differences in attendance were examined by t tests for each of the 7 years and for the composite; the results of these analyses are shown in Table 8.

During the first 5 years of life, attendance at the feeding stations in the Atole villages was significantly greater than in the Fresco villages; this pattern was reversed in year 7, when attendance became higher in the Fresco villages. It is consequently possible that any differences in outcome found between Atole and Fresco villages may be explained in part by attendance rather than by nutritional differences. The findings also suggest that the

TABLE 8

MEAN NUMBER OF TIMES ATOLE AND FRESCO SUBJECTS ATTENDED A FEEDING
STATION BY YEAR OF PARTICIPATION

Attendance Year	N	M	SD	t
Year 1:				
Atole	340	179.51	109.56	15.42***
Fresco	318	71.98	65.15	
Year 2:				
Atole	395	191.52	110.68	9.26***
Fresco	369	123.40	92.42	
Year 3:				
Atole	440	207.34	107.91	7.52***
Fresco	415	153.14	102.64	
Year 4:				
Atole	510	203.84	103.55	3.95***
Fresco	462	177.79	101.75	
Year 5:				
Atole	546	206.27	100.10	2.87**
Fresco	520	188.29	103.97	
Year 6:				
Atole	556	188.15	98.53	.08
Fresco	534	187.69	104.97	
Year 7:				
Atole	515	182.78	99.23	2.51**
Fresco	505	198.91	105.88	
ATTEND:[a]				
Atole	772	833.21	643.67	4.20***
Fresco	728	704.26	543.28	

[a] Attendance summed over all participation years.
** $p < .01$.
*** $p < .001$.

motivation for going to the respective treatment centers may have differed. Thus, mothers in Atole villages may have taken their small children more frequently to the treatment center in the belief that the Atole had nutritional benefits, while mothers in the Fresco villages may not have perceived the Fresco as being advantageous to their children. Conversely, since older children were able to attend on their own, the higher attendance in Fresco villages at age 7 might be explained by the children's preference for the taste of the Fresco over the Atole.

Attendance and SES Measures

In general, the associations in both Atole and Fresco villages between SES indices and the attendance measures were negative, small, and often not statistically different from zero. Mother's years of schooling was the SES variable most highly correlated with attendance, and the correlations reached significant levels at 1, 2, and 3 years in the Atole villages ($r = -.20$, $-.21$, and $-.23$, respectively).

Attendance and Preschool Factor Scores

Correlational analyses yielded significant positive associations (ranging from $r = .11$ to $r = .28$) between Factor 1 scores (see Chap. II) obtained at 3, 4, 5, and 7 years and attendance at most ages in the Fresco villages. Conversely, in the Atole villages, the associations were small and nonsignificant.

Significant correlations were obtained in the Fresco villages between attendance at 2, 3, and 4 years of age and Factor 2 scores at age 3 years ($r = .15, .18,$ and $.22$, respectively). In the Atole villages, the only significant associations reflected a negative relation (ranging from $r = -.10$ to $r = -.21$) between attendance from 1 to 6 years and Factor 2 scores at age 5 years.

Subsequent regression analyses of the preschool factor scores on attendance, controlling for socioeconomic status, indicated that attendance was significantly associated with Factor 1 scores and that these associations differed by treatment. The coefficients suggested that, for every 1,000 days of attendance in the Fresco villages, the factor score increased by four-tenths of a standard deviation, reflecting a moderate effect size. At the average rate of attendance at the supplementation centers—which was 182 days per year—5.5 years would be required to observe an effect size of this magnitude.

In summary, between-village differences in attendance did exist. In comparison to the Fresco sites, subjects in the Atole villages attended the station significantly more often during the first 5 years of life. The opposite held for the oldest (7-year-old) children, who were more likely to attend the Fresco than the Atole stations. Attendance, in turn, maintained a different relation with test performance in the two groups, being positively related to the two Preschool Battery factor scores in the Fresco but not in the Atole villages. Although the probability of observing an effect of attendance was limited, we nevertheless decided that further analyses should control for the potential confounding of attendance.

The possible reasons for the observed differences in attendance are numerous, and it is likely that they varied across time as a function of the treatment and its interaction with the individuals. In terms of available data, a recent analysis of children's participation in the Guatemala study between 1969 and 1977 indicated that proximity to the feeding center and larger family size were significant predictors of attendance. Lower socioeconomic status also proved to be associated with attendance in Atole but not in Fresco villages (Schroeder, Kaplowitz, & Martorell, 1992).

Assumption of a True Treatment

Any test of the effects of a nutritional intervention on developmental outcomes is grounded in the assumption that an intervention in fact occurred. It is possible, however, that, even though subjects indeed consumed the supplement, they may have concurrently reduced their home intakes. If this were the case, then it is conceivable that the net intake of nutrients of the Atole and Fresco subjects did not in fact differ. Lechtig et al. (1975) examined this issue in connection with assessing the energy intake of pregnant women enrolled in the longitudinal study and concluded that the supplement did result in a net increase of total calories. Further, we also examined the dietary data of children whose high Atole intake placed them at particularly high risk of substitution and found that the energy intake from the home diets of subjects whose Atole supplement intake was above 200 kcal per day did not differ from that of those whose intake was below 200 kcal per day. Taken together, these results suggest that the supplement was not used as a substitute to replace home diet.

A second level of analysis aimed at establishing the presence of a nutritional experiment centers on whether variables known to be sensitive to changes in nutritional status did indeed change as expected. In the absence of laboratory data, the answer to this question can be found only in an analysis of physical growth. In the case of the Guatemala study, Martorell et al. (1980) reported that greater supplement intake was associated with improved growth in the length, weight, head circumference, and arm length of preschool-aged children.

In summary, we concluded that the Atole was indeed a nutrient intervention and that variables that are sensitive to nutritional status (e.g., growth) were, in fact, affected by the intervention.

Different Histories

Another potential threat to the internal validity of the study arises from differences in the history of each village, as well as of each subject, in the period between the time the study was initiated (1969) and the follow-up (1988). Of particular importance are any educational differences between villages and between subjects. By the time of the follow-up, all the subjects were past both the legal (7 years) and the average (8.3 years) age at which children first enroll in school. In the initial hypotheses of the follow-up study, we conjectured that, if observed, beneficial effects of the treatment would be consistent at the individual level across measures of school performance and psychoeducational test performance. In addition, given that schooling is an important contributor to the development of cognitive abilities (Ceci, 1991), any assessment of cognitive skills requires controlling for school experiences, particularly in light of the vast individual differences in levels of school performance among the village subjects.

One potential problem with this approach is that any of the possible differences between the schools could be responsible for differences attributed to the treatment. Data on school quality would provide information directly related to differences in performance achieved in different schools; however, data of this nature are unfortunately not available. Furthermore, with only one school per village, statistical control for between-school differences would not be possible even if the relevant data were on hand.

We do know that all four schools were of low quality. None had the administrative infrastructure that is common in the industrialized world, teachers had no more than a secondary education, classrooms included more than one grade, ages within a grade spanned several years, and the decisions as to who should be promoted were not based on standardized criteria.

Under such conditions, it is highly unlikely that cognitive skills and abilities would be the sole determinants of school advancement (Gorman & Pollitt, 1993). Furthermore, it has also been reported that certain school indicators varied as a function of work-related tasks and opportunities available in the given village (Balderston, 1981). We also know from the data on parents' education levels that both fathers and mothers from Fresco villages had attended school longer and were more likely to be literate than Atole mothers and fathers.

Data on different school indicators immediately point to sizable differences that favor the Fresco rather than the Atole villages. For example, at the school level, first-grade promotion rates in Fresco villages averaged .54 over an 8-year period (1975–1982), whereas the rate for Atole villages was only .37. Similarly, repetition and dropout rates were higher in Atole villages (.42 and .21, respectively) than in Fresco villages (.32 and .14). At the individual level, a higher percentage of Fresco subjects (94.8) enrolled in school than Atole subjects (88.3), and significant differences in the number of grades passed and failed and the maximum grade attained also favored Fresco villagers.

When taken together, these data suggest—albeit tentatively—that there were substantial differences between the village schools that would work in the opposite direction from that hypothesized on the basis of the intervention. We are aware of the fact that these comparisons are based on individual level data rather than more desirable independent school quality indicators and hence could be given alternative interpretations. The parents' education and literacy data, however, are consistent with and provide strong support for our interpretation of these data.

The final concern in establishing between-village equivalence is whether selective attrition and/or recruitment for the follow-up may have differentiated between the Atole and the Fresco sites. This issue is examined in the methods section of the following chapter.

SUMMARY

The issues raised in this chapter point to limitations in the original design of the longitudinal study as well as to additional considerations that result from the restrictions in the pool of data available for the follow-up. We have addressed each concern with the best of our knowledge and ability, given the limitations of the data. We feel confident that, in identifying the potential confounders, we have laid the most important concerns to rest; the specifics of the analytic strategy that we used to deal with these concerns are described in Chapter VI.

V. METHODS OF THE CROSS-SECTIONAL FOLLOW-UP

This chapter describes the sample of subjects included in the follow-up study and the methods used to assess three sets of variables: the social and economic background of the families, the schooling histories of the subjects within the formal educational system of the villages, and the subjects' performance on a battery of psychoeducational and information-processing tests in adolescence.[5]

SUBJECTS

As a result of a 1987 census, 1,704 subjects were identified as composing the potential sample for follow-up assessment in the behavioral area. Owing to the large number of outcome variables of interest and the amount of time needed to test each subject, the cohorts born prior to 1965 were excluded from this aspect of the follow-up study. The intent was to maximize the amount of information to be collected without loss of the theoretically most important cohorts; since cohorts born between 1962 and 1965 had received supplementation at a noncritical developmental period (age 4–7), these were considered to be of least theoretical interest.

Of the 1,704 subjects, 1,545 were residing in the villages, and, of those, 93% completed the battery of psychoeducational tests that were selected for the follow-up assessment. With the inclusion of individuals who had migrated out of the villages but who could be contacted for testing either in Guatemala City or in surrounding villages, coverage of all potential subjects decreased to approximately 83%. Additional data cleaning resulted in the elimination of approximately 30 subjects from the psychology battery. A breakdown of the final number of subjects available for the follow-up psychoeducational tests is presented in Figure 3.

---

[5] Caroline Heckathorn was responsible for the analysis of the data on reliability and validity. We gratefully acknowledge her contributions to this chapter.

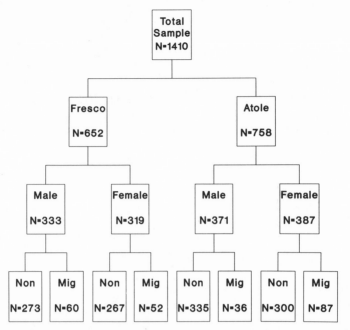

Fig. 3.—Breakdown of the follow-up sample (sample sizes available for a given analysis vary as a function of outcome variable and covariate). Non = nonmigratory, residing in the village. Mig = migratory, not residing in the village.

Comparisons of participants and nonparticipants allow us to make some inferences regarding the representativeness of the follow-up sample. Participants in the follow-up had higher mean birth weights, were less frequently ill with diarrhea from birth to 3 years of life, and had higher average energy intakes from the supplement during the first 3 years of life than nonparticipants (Rivera & Castro, 1990). However, this difference existed in both the Atole and the Fresco villages, and the rate of participation among village residents was similar in both types of sites (94% and 93% for females and 86% and 84% for males in the Atole and Fresco villages, respectively).

In addition, the percentage of migrants—defined as subjects not living in the villages at the time of the follow-up—from the entire sample was also similar in the Atole (32.7%, $N = 377$) and the Fresco (34.4%, $N = 350$) sites (Rivera & Castro, 1990), as was the proportion of migrants who participated in the follow-up (41.4% in the Fresco and 40.0% in the Atole villages).

Comparisons of the results as a function of migratory status, and with migrants removed from analyses, yielded two important pieces of information. First, although the migrants who enlisted in the follow-up performed significantly better than the nonmigrants on all psychoeducational tests, their performance was similar across Atole and Fresco subgroups. The only exception occurred on the Raven's Progressive Matrices test: migrants who were natives of the Fresco villages performed significantly better on this test than those from the Atole villages. When migrants were removed from the main analyses, the results of these remained virtually unchanged. Thus, although the follow-up sample may have been slightly better off than the entire longitudinal sample and migrants may be better off than nonmigrants, none of the observed sampling differences should modify any observed treatment effects.

Ideally, the entire sample would be broken down by cohorts defined by periods of exposure (e.g., prenatal only, postnatal only, first 2 years of life) so as to assess whether developmental period and duration of exposure modified the effects of the nutrient supplement; however, restrictions of statistical power precluded such an approach.[6] Accordingly, our analyses focus on the entire sample and on a cohort of maximum exposure, that is, subjects who were exposed to the treatment during gestation and for at least the first 2 years of postnatal life. Sample sizes in these two cohorts are large, with power to detect even small effects (power = .98 for an effect size greater than .20). In addition, the final analyses included a "late" cohort whose age at first exposure was 24 months or older (power = .74 for an effect size of .25).

The composition of the follow-up sample according to age of exposure and its duration is presented diagrammatically in Figure 4. The cohort of maximum exposure includes all subjects who received nutritional treatment during a period of accelerated brain growth, which represents a sensitive, if not the most sensitive, period when considering the effects of a nutritional intervention. These subjects were born between 1970 and 1974 and ranged in age from 13 to 19 years at the time of the follow-up study. They represent the most suitable sample on which to test the effects of the treatment. By contrast, the cohort of late exposure, born during or prior to 1967, helps determine whether exposure during the period of accelerated brain growth is a necessary condition for treatment effects.

SOCIOECONOMIC INDICATORS

Census data from each of the four villages were collected prior to the initiation of the study (1967), in the midst of the supplementation period

---

[6] For subjects with prenatal exposure only, sample size was 77 (52 for tests requiring literacy). Estimated power for an effect size of .25 was 58 (42 for literate group). For subjects with postnatal exposure only, sample size was 30. Estimated power for effect size of .25 was 26.

Age of Exposure

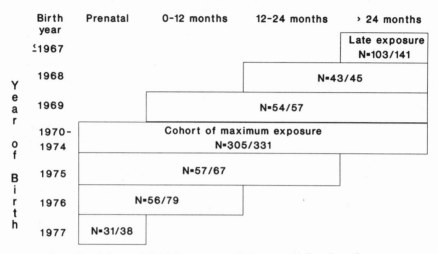

FIG. 4.—Breakdown of the follow-up sample by age and duration of exposure

(1974), and prior to the follow-up (1987). From these data, three indicators of socioeconomic status (SES) that reflect family wealth and potential for child stimulation were constructed: house quality, mothers' education, and fathers' occupation. Father's education was not included because the informants (mothers) often lacked knowledge about their husbands' schooling. In the final analyses, these indicators were standardized and summed to yield a single composite socioeconomic index.

For each census, all women over the age of 15 who had ever been married and all mothers in each village were interviewed, and information was obtained on each member of the nuclear family living in the household. The census forms for 1974 and 1987 were identical; the one used in 1967 was somewhat different but yielded comparable information. The informants also provided information about family structure, marital status, religion, number of pregnancies, number of live children, and relationship of household head to head of the extended family. Observations of the quality of the house were also made (e.g., type of walls, floor, and roof). For each family member, the parity, relationship to the rest of the family, birthdate, education, occupation (if over age 10), and date of change of status (death or migration) were coded. In addition, in 1987, when many of the subjects had started their own families, information about their families of origin was also recorded. Table 9 shows the number of families per village that were included in each round of the census as well as the total number of families for whom data were obtained at at least one of the three assessments.

TABLE 9

NUMBER OF FAMILIES WITH SES DATA BY YEAR OF CENSUS AND VILLAGE

	1967	1974	1987	Total[a]
Fresco 03	174	225	369	471
Atole 06	178	236	368	464
Fresco 08	132	187	254	325
Atole 14	110	136	237	281

NOTE.—Villages are identified by census codes.

[a] Number of families for whom data were obtained at any assessment date; new families formed in 1987 are included.

Construction of SES Measures

House Quality

In developing countries, it is often difficult to obtain accurate information on family income, a variable that traditionally has served as a proxy for a number of social-environmental variables that affect cognitive growth and educational development. This is particularly the case in rural agricultural communities and explains why indicators of house quality have often been used as proxies for income in such communities (e.g., Johnston, Low, de Baessa, & MacVean, 1987).

Nine variables describing house quality were assessed at each of the three census periods: an overall rating of the type of house (on a scale of 1–4); ownership of house (no = 0, yes = 1); number of rooms; type of floor (1–5); type of walls (1–7); type of roof (1–4); location of the kitchen (1–3); type of toilet (1–4); and number of possessions (1–6). In all instances, higher scale scores reflected the higher quality of the dwelling. Data were also available for type of water disposal, source of water, and presence of electricity. However, these variables were not used in the assessment of house quality because they tended to be village specific and contributed little to within-village variation.

To generate an index of within-village variation in house quality and of socially meaningful between-village differences, a factor analysis was performed to generate factor loadings for each assessment year. The nine variables were standardized within each village to allow for comparability across villages and then factor analyzed at each year using a principal components analysis. The results are shown in Table 10. Since the second principal component did not account for more than 13% of the variance at any year, it was dropped from further analyses; loadings on the first factor were similar at each time period.

In order to recapture between-village differences that were removed through standardization, final house quality scores were constructed by mul-

TABLE 10

FACTOR LOADINGS ON THE FIRST PRINCIPAL COMPONENTS
FACTOR OF THE NINE INDICES OF HOUSE QUALITY
(Using within-Village Standardized Scores)

Variable	1967	1974	1987
Possessions	.50	.53	.60
House	.84	.88	.88
Ownership	−.03	−.01	−.04
Rooms	.77	.74	.62
Floor	.51	.65	.82
Walls	.80	.83	.82
Roof	.52	.54	.56
Toilet	.32	.46	.55
Kitchen	.71	.64	.29
Eigenvalue	3.32	3.66	3.57
% variance	.37	.41	.40

tiplying the original individual raw scores by the factor loadings. An alternative approach, used in Ruel (1991), eliminated variables that varied systematically by village and derived the factor scores without multiplying the raw scores by the factor loadings. These scores, which were calculated for the 1974 and 1988 data, correlated at $r = .91$ and $.88$, respectively, with the scores that we used for analyses reported here.

Parents' Education

Parents' education has been consistently shown to be positively related to the cognitive development of the offspring (Sigman, Neumann, Jansen, & Bwibo, 1989). The mechanisms underlying this close-to-universal association are numerous, and they probably vary across cultures. In a variety of studies, parents' education has been positively related to frequency of educational opportunities available to the children, verbal stimulation provided to the offspring, and parents' aspirations for their children (Levine et al., 1991; Sigman et al., 1988; Sigman et al., 1989).

Informants reported parents' literacy (coded 0 = none, 1 = some) at all three census periods and parents' years of schooling in 1974 and 1987. The mean number of years of schooling in 1974 and 1987 was, respectively, .98 and 2.1 for mothers and 1.3 and 2.5 for fathers.

Parents' Occupation

Occupational status is a "carrier" variable that may be associated with income, status in the community, availability of resources, and family social-

TABLE 11

CORRELATION OF SES MEASURES OVER THE THREE CENSUS PERIODS

	1967–1974	1967–1987	1974–1987
House factor	.69**	.37**	.50**
	(466)	(360)	(533)
Mother:			
Literacy	.72**	.63**	.77**
	(429)	(326)	(491)
Education[a]			.80**
			(488)
Father:			
Literacy	.82**	.82**	.77**
	(380)	(282)	(433)
Education[a]			.73**
			(397)
Occupation	.36**	.27**	.37**
	(371)	(282)	(427)

NOTE.—Pearson product-moment correlation coefficients were computed for house quality and education and Spearman rank-order coefficients for literacy and occupation. Sample size is given in parentheses.

[a] Data are not available for 1967.

** $p < .01$.

ization practices. The indirect effects of parents' occupation on the cognitive development of children are thought to occur through the earning capacity of the parents and the consequent resources for stimulation that that earning capacity permits. Both mother's occupation and father's occupation were assessed; however, since only about 20% of women at the follow-up reported having an occupation, mother's occupation was excluded from further analyses.

There were six occupational categories listed in the 1967 census and 19 in the 1974 and 1987 censuses. For purposes of comparisons across years, the original 0–19 scales used in 1974 and 1987 were collapsed to be similar to the 1967 scale; these original and recoded scales are highly correlated ($r = .88$). In preliminary analyses, the recoded scale demonstrated adequate linear properties and was used in all subsequent statistical calculations as an ordinal variable.

Reliability of Measures

As shown in Table 11, most indicators remained stable over time. As expected, the highest correlations are obtained for variables that have little intraindividual variability and little expected change, such as years of school attainment, while the smallest values occur for variables that might be more likely to change over time, such as the characteristics of the family's home.

In subsequent, final analyses, indicators obtained in 1987 were used. An SES composite was created by summing three standardized variables: house factor score, father's occupation, and mother's schooling. As noted earlier, mother's occupation was dropped owing to its low occurrence, and father's education (as reported by the mother) was also excluded since the mothers often could not provide accurate information.

SCHOOLING VARIABLES

Five variables were generated from the individual schooling data: age at which the child entered school; number of times the child passed, failed, and withdrew; and the highest grade that the child reached. The data are shown in Table 12. On average, children began school more than a year after the expected age (i.e., 7 years for first grade), and some did so as late as at age 15 years. Children who attended school attained, on average, a level somewhat lower than the fourth grade (3.7), and failure was not uncommon (see Table 12). A more complete description of the Guatemalan educational system and of the measures of school efficiency in these villages is provided elsewhere (Gorman & Pollitt, 1992).

THE PSYCHOLOGICAL TEST BATTERY

With the intention of assessing two distinct aspects of cognition, two psychological test batteries were used in the follow-up. The psychoeducational test battery included Raven's Progressive Matrices and tests of complex intellectual aptitudes, abilities, and achievements that are heavily influenced by experience, education, and cultural upbringing. Illustrative of the latter are two standardized tests of reading and vocabulary and a knowl-

TABLE 12

Means, Standard Deviations, and Ranges of the School Variables Coded for the Guatemalan Adolescent Population

Variable	N	Range	M	SD
Age at entry	1,083	6.00–15.00	8.36	1.37
Pass	1,056	0–7.00	3.63	2.12
Fail	1,056	0–6.00	1.03	1.05
Withdrawals	1,056	0–4.00	.17	.46
Highest grade reached	1,089	0–6.00	3.72	2.07

edge test that was developed locally. The theoretical justification for the selection of these tests was the expectation that proficiency in reading and vocabulary and breadth of general knowledge will determine in part the potential that an adolescent or a young adult has to contribute to his or her community's social and economic development. Our particular concern was whether the nutritional supplement made a difference in terms of the crystallization of those mental abilities.

The second test battery included elementary cognitive tasks, such as simple and choice reaction time (RT), that measure a single attribute of information processing: speed. A paired associates test was also included in this battery. The between-subject variability in RT tests is generally not accounted for by schooling and cultural background, yet test performance still maintains a low-level correlation (r's ranging from $-.10$ to $-.30$) with g or a general ability factor. Theoreticians currently claim that RT is a sensitive indicator of differences in brain function (Eysenck, 1986; Jensen, 1991; Vernon, 1987). In the present study, inclusion of these tests was justified by the assumption that RT would be particularly sensitive to the effects of nutrition on central nervous system activity.

The tests included in the two batteries and their psychometric properties are described below.

Psychoeducational Tests

The battery included tests of literacy, numeracy, and general knowledge, two standardized educational achievement tests, and Raven's Progressive Matrices (RPM). The achievement tests were part of the Interamerican Series originally designed to assess reading abilities of Spanish-speaking children in Texas (Manuel, 1967).

Tests of literacy, numeracy, and general knowledge were administered individually by four trained testers. The achievement and intelligence tests were administered either individually or in a group, depending on subject availability, time, and logistical constraints. All the testers were females with certification as primary school teachers, and they came from Guatemala City or from a medium-sized town located near the villages. Testers received extensive training by both Guatemalan and U.S. psychologists during pretesting and the pilot study.

Interrater reliability was calculated for literacy, numeracy, and general knowledge tests on the basis of four testing sessions with five raters (four testers and the psychologist) at each session. Percentage agreement varied between 86% and 100% for literacy, 97% and 100% for numeracy, and 94% and 100% for general knowledge.

Literacy

The literacy test consisted of two parts: a preliteracy measure of knowledge of letters, syllables, words, and short phrases and a reading test based on material familiar to the subjects. All subjects who reported having achieved 4 or fewer years of schooling were given the preliteracy test. Subjects who achieved between 4 and 6 years of schooling were asked to read the headline of a newspaper article aloud ("Futbol Guatemalteco bien representado en Caracas"). If mistakes were made in word recognition or pronunciation, then the preliteracy test was administered. Subjects who achieved more than 6 years of schooling were presumed to be literate.

The preliteracy test was scored on a four-point scale as follows: 1 = unable to complete prereading test, suspended; 2 = completed test with at least five errors, suspended; 3 = completed test with less than five errors, continued; 4 = only reading test, not preliteracy test, administered.

The reading test consisted of 19 questions about two different sets of stimuli: a *cedula* (identification card) and related personal data, and a newspaper article about a soccer game. For each stimulus, subjects were asked to read a short paragraph and then respond verbally to a series of questions regarding the information they had read. Coding was done by individual testers, and scoring was based on the total number of correct answers.

Numeracy

Subjects were asked to read aloud a list of numbers ranging from one to three digits, to read a list of prices of familiar articles, and to order a list of items sequentially by their prices. They were also shown three pictures reflecting common situations of buying, working, and transportation and asked to answer questions regarding costs, wages, fares, and distances that required the ability to add, subtract, multiply, or divide. There was a total of 41 items. Coding was done by individual testers, and scoring was based on the number of correct answers across all items.

Knowledge

The knowledge test consisted of 22 questions regarding common experiences related to school, work, transportation, legal-political structures, and health. Subjects were presented with situations that required either basic knowledge or simple decision-making skills to be understood. They were given three possible choices and asked to select the option that best answered the question. Coding was done by individual testers, and scoring reflected the total number of correct answers.

Achievement Tests

The Interamerican Reading Series is a standardized test that consists of three parts: level of comprehension, speed of comprehension, and vocabulary. As a result of the pilot study, and owing to time constraints, only the level of comprehension and vocabulary sections were included. All subjects who passed the preliteracy test, independent of years of schooling, were given the achievement tests. The tests were timed and given either individually or in a group of up to four subjects. Scores were the number of correct answers on each of the two scales.

Intelligence

Intelligence was assessed with Raven's Progressive Matrices (RPM), which consists of five scales (A–E) containing 12 items each. Data from pilot testing indicated very low variance on scales D and E; consequently, only scales A, B, and C were administered. The test was administered either individually or in a group, and scoring reflected the number of correct answers summed across the three scales.

Information Processing

Tests of simple, choice, and memory reaction time (RT) (Sternberg, 1966) composed the computerized battery of tests to assess information processing. In addition, a paired associates test was administered as part of this battery. The intent of the battery was to assess the speed with which an individual processed information in completing elementary cognitive tasks. As described below, two of the RT tests (i.e., choice and memory) also allowed an assessment of efficiency, that is, speed in relation to errors in response.

The computer programs for each test were designed for this study. Two Guatemalan testers from a medium-sized town centrally located near the villages were trained in the use of the computer program and data management. They had limited previous experience with computers but were trained extensively during both the pilot and the pretesting stages of the project.

Subjects to be tested were first introduced to the computer as if it were a television and a typewriter (both familiar objects). They were then given a chance to interact with the computer in a series of warm-up exercises prior to the administration of the test battery.

Simple Reaction Time

This task consisted of repeated presentations of a randomly selected stimulus (geometric figures such as a circle or triangle) at the center of a computer screen. The duration of the presentation was 0.5 sec, with an interstimulus interval that varied systematically between 0.5 and 2 sec. The subjects were instructed to press the bar of the keyboard as quickly as possible on appearance of the stimulus. The test consisted of 30 trials. The lapse between presentation of the target stimulus and the bar press was recorded for each response. The score was the mean reaction time across successful trials.

Choice Reaction Time/Accuracy

The task consisted of the presentation of 12 geometric figures, from which the subject selected two that then became target figures. A series of five figures (two target and three randomly selected from the initial set of 12) flashed on the screen sequentially with a display period of 0.5 sec and interstimulus intervals that varied systematically between 0.5 and 3 sec. Subjects were instructed to press the bar when the two target figures appeared in sequential order and to refrain from pressing the bar in response to any other figures or to the target figures when not presented in sequential order. The test consisted of 30 trials. In addition to calculating reaction time for all correct responses, the percentage positive (presence of motor response) and negative (inhibition of motor response) correct and the number of errors of omission and commission were also calculated. The standardized error and reaction time scores were then used to calculate measures of efficiency (total error score plus reaction time) and impulsivity (total error score minus reaction time) (Salkind & Wright, 1977). These two measures capture variation in style of response, taking into account both accuracy and speed. Large negative scores of the efficiency measure are interpreted as highly efficient responses, and large positive scores on the impulsivity index indicate impulsive responses.

Memory Task

This task follows Sternberg's (1966) paradigm. It consisted of the horizontal presentation of six geometric figures at the top of the computer screen for 3 sec; the figures then flashed off the screen, and a single target figure appeared at the center of the screen. Subjects had to press one of two different keys depending on whether the target figure was one of the six previously displayed figures or not. The test included 20 trials. As in the previous testing, scores consisted of reaction time, percentage of positive and negative correct, impulsivity, and efficiency.

Paired Associates

The task consisted of four pairs of randomly selected geometric figures that appeared at the top-left-hand corner of the screen for 5 sec. Figures were presented in two horizontal rows, paired vertically. Pairs were then flashed off the screen, and one of the four figures from the top row appeared in the middle of the screen; concurrently, the four figures from the bottom row appeared at the bottom of the screen. Each of the four figures was numbered (1–4). Subjects were requested to select the numbered figure that had been paired originally with the target figure by selecting the corresponding number on the keyboard. Each trial consisted of the presentation of four target figures (selected in random order). A bell rang after every correct response; incorrect answers received no feedback. The four pairs were consistent across all trials, while order of presentation was random. The test was completed after 30 trials or when all four pairs had been successfully matched on three consecutive trials. The score was the number of trials required to reach criterion.

Procedure

Each of the four villages was visited twice by a research team, once during the dry and once during the rainy season. The teams were rotated, and each team visited each village during one round of testing. The team stayed in the village for 3–9 weeks, depending on the size of the village and coverage rates. Teams were made up of a doctor, two anthropometrists, several interviewers for sociodemographic data collection, and three persons trained to collect the behavioral data: one person on each team administered the information-processing tests, and two administered the psychoeducational tests.

Subjects were asked to complete the series of psychoeducational and information-processing tests on two separate days; completion of both series in a single day was strongly discouraged and occurred infrequently. When administered on the same day, a break was given between the two testing sessions. The information-processing evaluation lasted approximately 30 min, while the psychoeducational assessment averaged 1 hour and 15 min. In the case of illiterate subjects, all tests were administered individually.

In each community, two staff members recruited subjects and made appointments for testing. All testing was conducted in houses in the community rented by the project and adapted appropriately. In addition to psychological assessments, subjects were given medical and anthropometric examinations and interviewed regarding sociodemographic characteristics.

Reliability of Tests

Test-Retest

Test-retest stability coefficients (Pearson product-moment correlation) for the psychoeducational and information-processing tests were assessed on a subsample of the Guatemalan adolescent study population ($N = 217$). Subjects who agreed to participate in retesting were assigned randomly to one or more of the information-processing and/or psychoeducational tests. The test-retest interim period ranged across subjects from 2 to 34 days, with a mean of 17.7 days (SD = 7.99). Tests with a test-retest stability coefficient of .40 or less were dropped from further analyses.

As shown in Table 13, the stability coefficients for the psychoeducational tests were high, ranging from .85 to .98. These coefficients are similar to published test-retest values for Raven's Progressive Matrices (Rath, 1959; Stinissen, 1956 [cited in Raven, Court, & Raven, 1984]) and the Interamerican Series (Manuel, 1967).

The stability coefficients for the reaction time and paired associates tests were also moderate to high. However, the other variables on the choice reaction test had coefficients under .40. The means and frequency distributions for these variables indicate that the test was not sufficiently difficult to capture individual differences; the frequency distribution of errors of commission, for example, showed the majority of subjects to have made few or no such errors.

Test-retest stability coefficients were also assessed on the basis of subsamples of subjects with longer versus shorter interims between testing. Differences in range of time between testing sessions did not significantly affect reliability coefficients.

Internal Homogeneity

Using the entire sample, Cronbach's alphas were calculated to assess the internal consistency of the RPM, the Interamerican Series, and the knowledge, numeracy, and reading tests. Alphas obtained for the RPM and the Interamerican vocabulary and reading tests were high (.79–.98) and similar to the internal consistency measures published for these tests in the

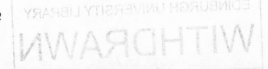

TABLE 13

Test-Retest Correlations of the Cognitive Measures Derived
for the Follow-Up Psychoeducational Battery Tests

	r		r
Psychoeducational battery tests:		Information-processing battery	
Raven (N = 88)	.87	tests:	
Knowledge (N = 87)	.88	Choice reaction time:	
Interamerican (N = 70):		Reaction time	.46
Reading	.85	% positive correct	.18[a]
Vocabulary	.87	% negative correct	.09[a]
Reading (N = 70)	.88	Efficiency	.23[a]
Literacy (N = 89)	.98	Impulsivity	.35[a]
Information-processing battery		Memory task (N = 70):	
tests:		Reaction time	.71
Numeracy (N = 89)	.90	% positive correct	.12[a]
Reaction time (N = 82)	.73	% negative correct	.72
Paired associates (N = 85):		Efficiency	.68
Trials to criterion	.47	Impulsivity	.72

[a] Dropped from further analysis.

literature (Arnold, 1969; Barahini, 1973; Stinissen, 1956 [cited in Raven et al., 1984]; Swinnen, 1958 [cited in Raven et al., 1984]).

The internal homogeneity of the numeracy, knowledge, and reading tests was of particular interest as these tests had been constructed specifically for use with the Guatemalan adolescents. The coefficient alpha for the numeracy test was .95; alphas for the knowledge (.67) and the reading (.75) tests were not as high, but we nevertheless considered them to fall within an acceptable range. Item deletions proved to increase the coefficient only marginally and hence were not considered necessary for subsequent analyses.

Tester Differences

Assessment of differences among testers was made by comparing mean scores obtained on each variable by each of the two information-processing testers and by each of the four psychoeducational testers.

As shown in Table 14, significant intertester differences were observed on all psychoeducational tests, except for the Interamerican reading test. A series of analyses was run to assess whether the differences were a function of length of time spent in the village, round of testing, systematic disposition of an individual tester, or teams of testers (since two testers were always working in each village together). The results suggest that the differences were more likely to be related to teams rather than to individual testers and that they were not systematic—no one tester appeared to be biasing the

TABLE 14

	TESTER				F VALUES
	1	2	3	4	
Literacy	3.42^a	$3.30^{a,b}$	3.22^b	3.05^c	6.57***
Reading	14.62^c	14.72^c	16.58^a	15.75^b	19.44***
Raven's Matrices	11.58^a	10.66^b	11.36^a	$11.01^{a,b}$	2.62*
Numeracy	33.33^a	30.82^b	$32.66^{a,b}$	31.91^b	5.55***
Knowledge	13.86^a	$13.59^{a,b}$	13.04^c	$13.32^{b,c}$	3.64**
Interamerican:					
Reading	17.34^a	17.03^a	17.07^a	16.69^a	.63
Vocabulary	25.02^b	25.07^b	26.75^a	26.43^a	3.63**

NOTE.—Duncan test; means with the same letter are not significantly different. $df(3, 1,405)$ for literacy, numeracy, knowledge, and RPM; $df(3, 1,052)$ for reading and Interamerican reading and vocabulary.

* $p < .05$.
** $p < .01$.
*** $p < .001$.

results in a specific direction. Nevertheless, because some of these differences were large and potentially capable of affecting findings on the effects of treatment, final analyses of the psychoeducational outcomes were run both with and without controlling for testers. Comparisons of results indicated that none of the treatment effects were modified significantly by tester variation.

Among the information-processing tests, the only scores on which significant tester differences were obtained were the choice reaction time and memory reaction time variables. These differences, however, were not large (.028 and .09 sec, respectively), suggesting that their statistical significance can possibly be attributed to the large sample size and does not represent behaviorally meaningful differences between testers.

Validity

To assess construct validity, a factor analysis was conducted to test the original assumption that the overall battery of tests assessed two distinct domains of cognition: complex intellectual aptitudes, abilities, and educational achievements and elementary aspects of information processing. Factor loadings obtained from a factor analysis with varimax rotation performed on the full set of variables showed that all the psychoeducational tests loaded strongly on the first factor, which reflects an overall, general abilities factor (see Table 15). Factor 2 loaded most heavily with two of the reaction time variables, and Factor 3 loaded a memory variable. Factor 4 included the number of trials to reach criterion on the paired associates test

TABLE 15

FACTOR LOADINGS OF ADOLESCENT COGNITIVE OUTCOME VARIABLES

OUTCOME VARIABLE	FACTOR			
	1	2	3	4
Raven's Matrices	.610			
Numeracy	.806			
Reading	.862			
Knowledge	.684			
Literacy	.664			
Interamerican vocabulary	.802			
Interamerican reading	.736			
Choice reaction time		.830		
Simple reaction time		.821		
Memory—reaction time				.708
Trials to criterion				−.647
Memory—% negative correct			.756	
Eigenvalues	3.90	1.40	1.23	1.05
% variance	51.4	18.5	16.1	13.8

and reaction time on the memory test. The composition of this last factor was somewhat unexpected as it had been assumed that memory reaction time would load with the other two reaction time measures.

The factor analysis supports the assumption that the psychoeducational and the information-processing test batteries assess two distinct cognitive domains. A clear division exists between Factor 1 (psychoeducational) and Factors 2, 3, and 4 (information processing). The factor-analytic separation of the simple and choice RT tests from the memory RT suggests that, in these subjects, the different measures of RT are not tapping the same cognitive functions and may, therefore, be sensitive to different types of influences. The existence of these distinct domains was confirmed with an oblique rotation.

Concurrent test validity was also addressed by calculating correlations between the test scores and the educational variables. Positive and statistically significant correlations—ranging from $r = .18$ to $r = .58$—were found between highest grade achieved and all the tests contained in the psychoeducational battery. Correlations between grade attainment and the information-processing variables were also statistically significant, but much lower, ranging from $-.10$ (simple RT) to $-.22$ (memory efficiency).

VI. RESULTS FROM THE CROSS-SECTIONAL FOLLOW-UP

Two sets of analyses were carried out to test for the effects of the dietary treatment on the psychoeducational and information-processing tests administered in 1988 and on the subjects' educational record. The first included all subjects for whom schooling data were available and assessed whether the nutritional treatment was associated with test performance. The second was restricted to subjects who never enrolled in school.

EFFECTS OF EXPERIMENTAL TREATMENT ON TEST SCORES

Statistical analyses were performed on both the entire sample and the "cohort of maximum exposure" (see Fig. 4 above) and then contrasted with results obtained for the cohort of late exposure. In keeping with previous work that has documented sex differences in both the biological and the behavioral response to supplementation (Engle & Levin, 1984), preliminary analyses tested for presence of any treatment × sex interactions. Since none emerged, all final analyses included sex as a main effect.

The data were analyzed in two steps. First, correlations were obtained across all subjects between the psychoeducational test scores and both SES indicators and school variables. Second, regression analyses were calculated on each cohort separately (e.g., entire sample, cohort of maximum exposure, cohort of late exposure) to assess the specific effects of the early supplementary feeding independent of the SES and school variables' effects.

Correlational Analyses

SES Indicators and Test Scores

Table 16 presents the correlations obtained between the SES indicators and the psychoeducational and information-processing test scores. All correlations with the former were significant ($p < .001$), ranging in size from

TABLE 16

CORRELATIONS BETWEEN ADOLESCENT OUTCOMES AND SOCIOECONOMIC INDICATORS

	SOCIOECONOMIC INDICATORS		
	House Quality	Mother's Education	Father's Occupation
Psychoeducational:			
Literacy	.31***	.27***	.16***
Reading	.15***	.19***	.15***
Numeracy	.28***	.29***	.20***
Knowledge	.28***	.30***	.25***
Raven's Matrices	.25***	.21***	.22***
Interamerican:			
Reading	.39***	.27***	.32***
Vocabulary	.35***	.25***	.27***
Information processing:			
Reaction time:			
Simple	−.05	−.06*	−.02
Choice	−.09**	−.04	−.01
Memory	−.07**	−.03	−.04
Trials to criterion	−.15***	−.11***	−.11***
Impulsivity	−.05	−.06*	−.03
Efficiency	−.14***	−.10***	−.07**
% negative correct	.13***	.09**	.06

NOTE.—Sample sizes range from 1,162 to 1,281 for all tests, except reading tests (range = 864–952) and paired associates (range = 948–1,046).

* $p < .05$.
** $p < .01$.
*** $p < .001$.

$r = .15$ to $r = .39$; higher SES was associated with higher test performance. Similarly, correlations with the information-processing tests were in the predicted direction; however, they were generally smaller than those involving the psychoeducational tests, and only 13 of 27 coefficients were statistically significant.

Schooling and Test Scores

Age of entry into school correlated at a statistically significant level with all the psychoeducational test scores (see Table 17); the earlier the enrollment, the better the performance. As would be expected, in the case of the information-processing tasks, fewer coefficients (four of seven) were statistically significant, and their magnitude was much smaller (range from −0.10 to 0.16 for significant coefficients).

All correlations between the other school performance variables and psychoeducational test scores were statistically significant; as in the case of the SES indicators, the correlations with the information-processing vari-

TABLE 17

CORRELATIONS BETWEEN SCHOOLING VARIABLES AND ADOLESCENT OUTCOMES

	SCHOOLING VARIABLES			
	Age at Entry	Pass	Fail	Highest Grade
Psychoeducational:				
Literacy	−.36***	.69***	−.17***	.58***
Reading	−.24***	.40***	−.19***	.22***
Numeracy	−.33***	.61***	−.23***	.50***
Knowledge	−.20***	.39***	−.19***	.29***
Raven's Matrices	−.25***	.29***	−.20***	.21***
Interamerican:				
Reading	−.25***	.33***	−.20***	.18***
Vocabulary	−.27***	.36***	−.18***	.22***
Information processing:				
Reaction time:				
Simple	.02	−.09**	.02	−.03
Choice	.04	−.05	−.02	−.03
Memory	.11***	−.14***	.01	−.15***
Trials to criterion	.11***	−.13***	.05	−.10**
Impulsivity	.01	−.08**	.06*	−.02
Efficiency	.16***	−.27***	.08**	−.22***
% negative correct	−.10***	.23***	−.08**	.17***

* $p < .05$.
** $p < .01$.
*** $p < .001$.

ables were, generally, smaller, and only 65% of them (13 of 21) reached statistical significance.

In sum, bivariate associations between test performance and SES and between test performance and schooling were in the expected directions. In keeping with theoretical assumptions, the psychoeducational test battery was more sensitive to environmental factors (e.g., SES and schooling variables) than was the information-processing test battery.

Hierarchical Regression Analyses

Analytic Strategy

The main question raised in this *Monograph* is whether exposure to Atole had a differential effect on cognition in adolescence than exposure to Fresco. At issue is not only whether early malnutrition had developmental consequences but also whether early nutrient supplementation had preventative effects. Data analyses could be selectively focused on the presence or absence of main effects to address this issue; however, from a developmental perspective, such an approach is far too restrictive. It fails to consider the possibility of differential effects of treatment that may be related to particular characteristics of the population, and it disregards these data's potential for making a theoretical contribution to our understanding of cognitive development.

Adopting a more sophisticated approach, the data were analyzed using a hierarchical regression model. All independent variables were standardized. As in the correlational analysis, the 1987 data were selected for use as socioeconomic indicators, and a composite SES score was created by summing mother's education, father's occupation, and house quality index. Individual characteristics (sex, age, and attendance with consumption partialed out) were entered first, followed by the SES composite score, then the two school variables (age at entry and maximum grade), and, finally, treatment. In this way, we were able to calculate the amount of variance accounted for by the different types of predictors. In a subsequent step, two interaction terms were entered—treatment × maximum grade and treatment × SES. The results indicate the percentage of variance accounted for (R^2) and the F values and regression coefficients for each variable in the step in which it was entered, controlling for all other variables entered prior to this step.

The order in which we entered variables was based on the following basic assumptions: (i) Between-village differences in SES variables overlap with experimental treatment effects and could therefore account for some effects that might otherwise be attributed to treatment. (ii) Level-of-schooling variables have direct effects on the outcome variables and intervene in the relation between experimental treatment and outcome. (iii) Experimental treatment has direct effects on the outcome variables independent of all other effects that may be evident.

A three-way interaction term (treatment × SES × maximum grade) was also entered into the models; the results of these analyses are mentioned only where a significant three-way interaction was obtained. Similarly, since the focus of the analyses was on the effects of the treatment, presentation of results is limited to those SES × maximum grade interactions that were statistically significant. Since none of the treatment × sex or treatment × age interactive terms were shown to be statistically significant by preliminary analyses, they were dropped from the final model.

Entire Sample

Psychoeducational test performance.—Table 18 presents a summary of the results of the regression analyses. In general, males outperformed females on the psychoeducational tests (e.g., reading, numeracy, and RPM). There was also a significant main effect of age on all but the literacy test—older

59

TABLE 18

RESULTS OF HIERARCHICAL REGRESSION ANALYSES FOR THE ENTIRE SAMPLE
ON THE PSYCHOEDUCATIONAL TESTS

Step and Variables	R^2	Model F	F to enter	Parameter Estimate	Direction of Effect Favors:
Numeracy:					
1. Sex	.07	21.29***	13.14***	−1.901	Males
Age			41.53***	1.227	Older
Attendance[a]			9.19**	.894	Higher
2. SES	.15	37.07***	78.69***	1.079	Higher
3. Age at entry	.46	120.17***	146.73***	−.735	Younger
Max grade			342.30***	4.362	Higher
4. Treatment (Rx)	.47	108.30***	20.63***	1.924	Atole
5. Rx × grade	.49	82.74***	2.73		
Rx × SES			8.12**		
Grade × SES			27.38***		
Knowledge:					
1. Sex	.21	74.93***	3.47	−.419	...
Age			218.31***	1.479	Older
Attendance[a]			3.00	.212	...
2. SES	.26	77.23***	66.98***	.416	Higher
3. Age at entry	.37	85.92***	69.60***	−.413	Younger
Max grade			83.06***	1.036	Higher
4. Treatment (Rx)	.39	77.21***	16.01***	.819	Atole
5. Rx × grade	.39	60.83***	.38		
Rx × SES			4.69*		
Vocabulary:					
1. Sex	.06	14.36***	1.45	−.705	...
Age			41.37***	1.818	Older
Attendance[a]			.25	.164	...
2. SES	.14	27.56***	63.19***	1.087	Higher
3. Age at entry	.26	39.65***	50.42***	−1.153	Younger
Max grade			59.55***	2.742	Higher
4. Treatment (Rx)	.31	42.78***	45.72***	3.717	Atole
5. Rx × grade	.32	35.55***	2.45		
Rx × SES			12.34***		
Reading achievement:					
1. Sex	.05	11.01***	.01	−.038	...
Age			32.59***	1.017	Older
Attendance[a]			.42	.139	...
2. SES	.13	25.24***	64.80***	.709	Higher
3. Age at entry	.22	31.76***	35.64***	−.634	Younger
Max grade			42.57***	1.525	Higher
4. Treatment (Rx)	.25	32.20***	27.33***	1.915	Atole
5. Rx × grade	.29		9.50**		
Rx × SES		29.99***	24.30***		
Raven's Progressive Matrices:					
1. Sex	.07	23.24***	39.80***	−1.801	Males
Age			25.88***	.563	Older
Attendance[a]			4.04*	.326	Higher
2. SES	.11	27.12***	35.96***	.412	Higher
3. Age at entry	.16	27.26***	21.24***	−.308	Younger
Max grade			27.91***	.854	Higher
4. Treatment (Rx)	.16	23.37***	.17	.121	...

TABLE 18 (*Continued*)

Step and Variables	R^2	Model F	F to enter	Parameter Estimate	Direction of Effect Favors:
Raven's Progressive Matrices:					
5. Rx × grade	.17	18.91***	.22		
Rx × SES			5.67*		
Grade × SES			.00		
6. Rx × grade × SES	.17	15.94***	4.62*		
Literacy:					
1. Sex	.02	7.30***	.61	−.057	...
Age			.61	−.060	...
Attendance[a]			20.67***	.178	Higher
2. SES	.10	24.85***	75.64***	.140	Higher
3. Age at entry	.54	166.40***	179.11***	−.044	Younger
Max grade			627.23**	.705	Higher
4. Treatment (Rx)	.54	143.53***	3.45†	.095	Atole
5. Rx × grade	.56	109.46***	2.98		
Rx × SES			.08		
Grade × SES			40.01***		
Reading:					
1. Sex	.15	40.39***	25.75***	−1.343	Males
Age			90.09***	1.092	Older
Attendance[a]			5.32*	.346	Higher
2. SES	.17	33.59**	11.35***	.217	Higher
3. Age at entry	.31	51.36***	77.29***	−.735	Younger
Max grade			67.88***	1.345	Higher
4. Treatment (Rx)	.31	43.96**	.03	.047	...
5. Rx × grade	.32	34.65***	.80		
Rx × SES			2.67		

NOTE.—Sample sizes for the entire sample range from 678 to 868.
[a] Attendance is the residual value after regressing attendance on consumption.
† $p < .10$.   ** $p < .01$.
* $p < .05$.   *** $p < .001$.

adolescents performed consistently better than younger ones. Likewise, the residual of attendance (after partialing out consumption) was positively associated with test performance, reaching statistical significance on three of the seven outcome variables (reading, numeracy, and RPM). As would be expected, there were main effects of SES, age of entry in school, and maximum grade attained: the higher the SES level, the younger the age at entry, and the higher the grade attained in school, the higher the test scores.

After controlling for potential confounders (in Steps 1–3), there was a main effect of treatment on the numeracy, knowledge, and Interamerican vocabulary and reading achievement tests; in all instances, the difference favored the Atole group. However, in each of these cases, the interactive term treatment × SES (Step 5) was statistically significant; this interactive term was also significant in the case of the Progressive Matrices test. The independent estimates of the slopes for the Atole and the Fresco groups on each of these five tests showed a significant positive slope for the Fresco but not for the Atole group. Figure 5 illustrates the pattern of the relations observed in each of these interactions. Thus, in the Fresco villages, test performance improved as SES improved, whereas no relation between SES and test performance existed in the Atole villages.

In addition, there was a significant maximum grade × treatment interaction on the reading achievement score; this interaction is plotted in Figure 6. In this case, both slopes were statistically significant, but the relation within the Atole group was stronger ($b = 2.445$, $p < .001$) than in the Fresco group ($b = .827$, $p < .05$). In other words, Atole children in the upper percentiles of grade attainment scored significantly higher than Fresco children, whereas no treatment differences were observed among children at the lowest end of the grade attainment distribution.

Significant SES × maximum grade interactions were obtained on the numeracy and literacy tests (see Table 18 above). In both cases, the significant positive relation between grade attainment and the outcomes at all levels of SES became less strong as SES levels increased; thus, subjects from low socioeconomic backgrounds showed a stronger relation between level of schooling and outcome.

Finally, there was a significant three-way interaction ($F = 4.62$, $p < .05$) on RPM. When the grade × SES interactions on this measure were explored separately for Atole and Fresco villages, neither interaction was statistically significant. However, in Atole villages, there was a positive relation between SES and RPM within the highest levels of grade attainment ($b = .274$, $p = .05$) but no relation when the attained grade level was low. Conversely, in Fresco villages, the relation between SES and RPM was significant at low levels of grade attainment ($b = .502$, $p < .0003$) but not at higher levels ($b = .245$, $p < .07$).

In sum, significant treatment effects were observed on four of the psychoeducational outcomes. Treatment × SES interactions were significant on five outcomes, indicating that the significant differences between Atole and Fresco subjects increased as socioeconomic status declined. Treatment × grade attained interactions revealed that the benefits of Atole were strongest for those children reaching a higher maximum grade.

Information processing.—As was true for the psychoeducational tests, on most information-processing tasks, males outperformed females (i.e., simple and choice reaction time, percentage negative correct, impulsivity, and efficiency on the memory task). Similarly, SES and both school measures were associated with performance on paired associates, memory reaction time, percentage negative correct, and efficiency—in the expected direction.

Of the seven analyses of information-processing outcomes (Table 19), there were two significant main effects of the treatment. Atole subjects per-

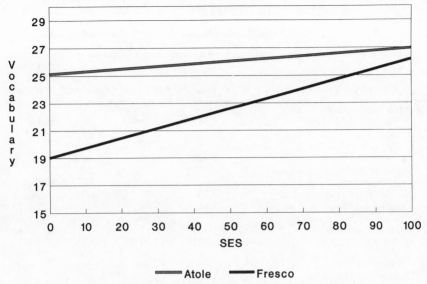

FIG. 5.—SES × treatment interaction for vocabulary for the entire sample

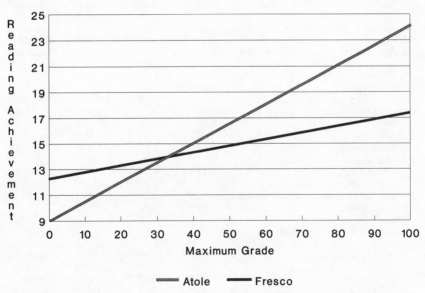

FIG. 6.—Maximum grade × treatment interaction for reading achievement in the entire sample.

TABLE 19

RESULTS OF HIERARCHICAL REGRESSION ANALYSES FOR THE ENTIRE SAMPLE
ON THE INFORMATION-PROCESSING TESTS

Step and Variables	R^2	Model F	F to enter	Parameter Estimate	Direction of Effect Favors:
Simple reaction time:					
1. Sex	.02	4.58**	12.20***	.021	Males
Age			.57	−.001	...
Attendance[a]			.98	−.003	...
2. SES	.02	3.72**	1.14	−.002	...
3. Age at entry	.02	3.15**	.11	−.002	...
Max grade			3.89*	−.007	Higher
4. Treatment (Rx)	.02	2.76**	.37	−.004	...
5. Rx × grade	.02	2.33**	1.54		
Rx × SES			.14		
Choice reaction time:					
1. Sex	.01	3.90**	11.29***	.038	Males
Age			.31	.002	...
Attendance[a]			.08	.002	...
2. SES	.02	3.76**	3.31	−.005	...
3. Age at entry	.02	2.62*	.01	−.002	...
Max grade			.73	−.006	...
4. Treatment (Rx)	.02	2.41*	1.15	−.013	...
5. Rx × grade	.02	1.98*	.92		...
Rx × SES			.04		...
Paired associates trials to criterion:					
1. Sex	.006	1.51	3.24	.903	...
Age			.91	−.332	...
Attendance[a]			.39	.187	...
2. SES	.02	4.48***	13.30***	−.455	Higher
3. Age at entry	.04	5.55***	6.20**	.335	Younger
Max grade			8.83**	−.874	Higher
4. Treatment (Rx)	.05	4.92***	1.18	−.588	...
5. Rx × grade	.05	4.42***	.11		
Rx × SES			5.03*		
Memory reaction time:					
1. Sex	.005	1.48	.25	−.036	...
Age			3.07	.090	...
Attendance[a]			1.11	−.046	...
2. SES	.01	2.37*	5.02*	−.042	Higher
3. Age at entry	.04	5.41***	6.61**	.031	Younger
Max grade			16.12***	−.180	Higher
4. Treatment (Rx)	.05	5.92***	8.72**	−.241	Atole
5. Rx × grade	.05	4.61***	.06		
Rx × SES			.05		
% negative correct on memory task:					
1. Sex	.04	11.93***	25.26***	−.083	Males
Age			.55	−.009	...
Attendance[a]			9.98**	.030	Higher
2. SES	.05	10.54***	6.15**	.010	Higher

TABLE 19 (*Continued*)

Step and Variables	R^2	Model F	F to enter	Parameter Estimate	Direction of Effect Favors:
% negative correct on memory task:					
3. Age at entry	.08	12.28***	7.71**	−.006	Younger
Max grade			22.39***	.046	Higher
4. Treatment (Rx)	.08	10.66***	.93	.017	...
5. Rx × grade	.08	8.34***	.53		
Rx × SES			.03		
Impulsivity on memory task:					
1. Sex	.02	6.78***	12.65***	.341	Males
Age			4.90*	−.062	Older
Attendance[a]			2.79	−.091	...
2. SES	.02	5.12***	.18	−.010	...
3. Age at entry	.02	3.44**	.07	.006	...
Max grade			.12	−.020	...
4. Treatment (Rx)	.03	3.33**	2.61	.168	...
5. Rx × grade	.03	2.62**	.00		
Rx × SES			.32		
Efficiency on memory task:					
1. Sex	.02	5.26***	6.33**	.270	Males
Age			3.69*	.117	Older
Attendance[a]			9.19**	−.182	Higher
2. SES	.03	7.27***	13.09***	−.093	Higher
3. Age at entry	.09	14.33***	16.25***	.067	Younger
Max grade			38.79***	−.377	Higher
4. Treatment (Rx)	.10	13.50***	7.87**	−.308	Atole
5. Rx × grade	.10	10.51***	.19		
Rx × SES			.04		

NOTE.—Sample sizes for the entire sample range from 678 to 878.

[a] Attendance is the residual value after regressing attendance on consumption.

* $p < .05$.
** $p < .01$.
*** $p < .001$.

formed faster and more efficiently on the memory task than those exposed to Fresco.

In addition, there was one treatment × SES interaction on the paired associates task. Whereas SES was not associated with performance in the Atole subjects, in Fresco villages there was a significant inverse relation ($b = −.569$, $p < .05$). As SES improved, fewer trials were necessary to reach criterion for the Fresco subjects.

In sum, when significant, treatment effects favored Atole subjects. Compared to the observed effects on psychoeducational test performance, treatment effects were less consistently observed across outcomes and tended to be main rather than interactive effects.

Cohort of Maximum Exposure

Psychoeducational tests.—As shown in Table 20, the results of analyses restricted to this cohort closely resembled those obtained for the entire sample. Test performance tended to be better for older subjects, males, and those with higher levels of SES and grade attainment. There were main effects of treatment on numeracy, knowledge, and the Interamerican reading and vocabulary tests favoring Atole subjects. The interactions between treatment and SES were again statistically significant in the cases of numeracy, knowledge, RPM, and the Interamerican reading and vocabulary tests. The interactions for four of these outcomes (with the exception of reading, where there was a significant three-way interaction) are depicted in Figure 7. In all but the case of RPM, the slopes were statistically significant for the Fresco but not for the Atole group. At the lower ends of the SES distribution, Atole subjects performed significantly better than Fresco subjects; at higher levels of SES, there were no differences between Atole and Fresco subjects. On RPM, a slightly different pattern was observed: Atole children performed significantly better than Fresco children at the lowest end of the SES distribution (at or below the tenth percentile) but below Fresco children at its highest end (at or above the ninetieth percentile).

Treatment × maximum grade interactions were also observed on the reading and the two achievement tests. In all cases, slopes were positive and significant for Atole but not for Fresco subjects. On both achievement tests (for an illustration, see Fig. 8), differences between treatment groups increased with grade attainment, with children from Atole villages scoring significantly higher at the upper ends of the grade distribution than subjects exposed to Fresco. On the reading test (Fig. 9), Fresco subjects outperformed Atole subjects at the lower end of the distribution (at or below the twenty-fifth percentile), but there were no differences between groups in performance at the upper end of the grade distribution.

A grade × SES interaction was observed on the literacy test. As was true for the entire sample, the relation between grade attainment and literacy became weaker as SES improved, although, at all levels of SES, grade attainment was significantly and positively related to the outcome.

Finally, a significant three-way interaction was obtained on the Interamerican reading test. The SES × grade interaction was significant in Fresco but not Atole villages; within the Fresco villages, associations between SES and achievement were positive and significant for both low ($b = 1.885$, $p < .0001$) and high ($b = .834$, $p < .0001$) levels of grade attainment.

Information-processing tests.—Results obtained for the maximum exposure cohort were again similar to those for the entire sample (see Table 21). Gender (i.e., males), higher socioeconomic status, earlier school entry, and higher grade attainment were associated with enhanced performance on

TABLE 20

RESULTS OF HIERARCHICAL REGRESSION ANALYSES FOR THE COHORT OF MAXIMUM
EXPOSURE ON THE PSYCHOEDUCATIONAL TESTS

Step and Variables	R^2	Model F	F to enter	Parameter Estimate	Direction of Effects Favors:
Numeracy:					
1. Sex	.02	3.46*	2.12	−1.066	...
Age			6.69**	1.556	Older
Attendance[a]			1.55	.529	Higher
2. SES	.10	11.15***	33.42***	1.042	Higher
3. Age at entry	.46	57.06***	84.09***	−.721	Younger
Max grade			184.59**	4.456	Higher
4. Treatment (Rx)	.47	50.83***	7.75**	1.708	Atole
5. Rx × grade	.48	41.44***	.01		
Rx × SES			10.06***		
Knowledge:					
1. Sex	.06	8.71***	.17	.140	...
Age			25.42***	1.627	Older
Attendance[a]			.56	.135	...
2. SES	.12	13.95***	27.93***	.408	Higher
3. Age at entry	.24	21.55***	34.14***	−.481	Younger
Max grade			30.78***	.932	Higher
4. Treatment (Rx)	.26	20.04***	8.57**	.919	Atole
5. Rx × grade	.27	16.63**	.79		
Rx × SES			6.74**		
Raven's Progressive Matrices:					
1. Sex	.06	8.07***	19.40***	−1.844	Males
Age			4.32*	.793	Older
Attendance[a]			.50	.171	...
2. SES	.09	9.80***	14.19***	.396	Higher
3. Age at entry	.13	10.09***	6.59***	−.170	Younger
Max grade			13.06***	.871	Higher
4. Treatment (Rx)	.13	8.66***	.22	.212	...
5. Rx × grade	.15	8.05**	2.18		
Rx × SES			8.39**		
Reading achievement:					
1. Sex	.01	1.68*	.02	.038	...
Age			3.29**	1.624	Older
Attendance[a]			1.74	−.420	...
2. SES	.12	10.76***	37.43***	.845	Higher
3. Age at entry	.18	11.70***	12.67***	−.621	Younger
Max grade			11.58***	1.239	Higher
4. Treatment (Rx)	.22	13.47***	20.05***	2.558	Atole
5. Rx × grade	.29	14.43***	13.14***		
Rx × SES			14.91***		
Grade × SES			.10		
6. Rx × grade × SES	.30	12.75***	7.88**		
Vocabulary:					
1. Sex	.03	3.16*	.01	−.122	...
Age			8.01**	3.290	Older
Attendance[a]			1.48	−.571	...
2. SES	.11	10.66***	32.26***	1.168	Higher
3. Age at entry	.21	14.25***	18.98***	−1.064	Younger
Max grade			19.17***	2.327	Higher

TABLE 20 (*Continued*)

Step and Variables	R^2	Model F	F to enter	Parameter Estimate	Direction of Effects Favors:
Vocabulary:					
4. Treatment (Rx)	.26	16.20***	22.35***	3.930	Atole
5. Rx × grade	.30	15.13***	6.13**		
Rx × SES			11.28***		
Reading:					
1. Sex	.09	10.37***	8.83**	−1.152	Males
Age			21.95***	1.849	Older
Attendance[a]			.32	.121	. . .
2. SES	.10	8.94***	4.36*	.204	Higher
3. Age at entry	.28	21.20***	47.41**	−.848	Younger
Max grade			35.24***	1.412	Higher
4. Treatment (Rx)	.28	18.12***	.03	.062	Atole
5. Rx × grade	.30	15.22***	5.36*		
Rx × SES			2.49		
Literacy:					
1. Sex	.01	1.49	1.10	.096	. . .
Age			1.03	.016	. . .
Attendance[a]			2.32	.081	. . .
2. SES	.08	8.85***	30.61***	.125	Higher
3. Age at entry	.55	82.34***	102.52***	−.040	Younger
Max grade			319.76***	.666	Higher
4. Treatment (Rx)	.55	70.54***	.44	.047	. . .
5. Rx × grade	.56	52.25***	.54		
Rx × SES			.14		
Grade × SES			13.92***		

NOTE.—Sample sizes for the cohort of maximum exposure range from 335 to 416.

[a] Attendance is the residual value after regressing attendance on consumption.

* $p < .05$.

** $p < .01$.

*** $p < .001$.

the information-processing test battery. Three significant main effects of treatment were observed. Compared to Fresco subjects, Atole subjects reached criterion faster on the paired associates task and responded faster and more efficiently on the memory task.

Although one significant three-way interaction was obtained on the percentage negative correct on the memory task, when the relation between SES and grade was analyzed by treatment, the interactions were nonsignificant in both Atole and Fresco villages. There were no significant two-way interactions.

Overall Summary of Results

Focusing on treatment effects obtained in analyses of the psychoeducational tests, we see that, in both the entire sample and the cohort of maxi-

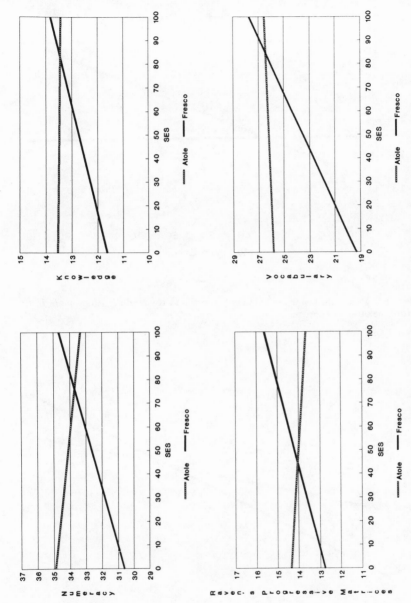

Fig. 7.—SES × treatment interactions for numeracy, RPM, knowledge, and vocabulary in the cohort of maximum exposure.

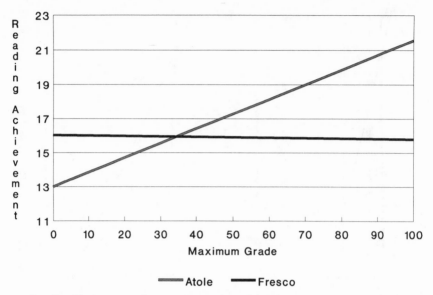

FIG. 8.—Maximum grade × treatment interaction for reading achievement in the cohort of maximum exposure.

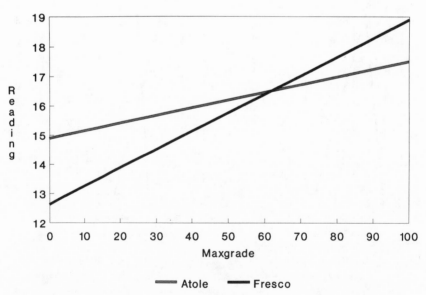

FIG. 9.—Maximum grade × treatment interaction for reading in the cohort of maximum exposure.

mum exposure, significant effects of Atole prevailed on the tests of numeracy, knowledge, vocabulary, and reading achievement. The percentage of variance accounted for by inclusion of the treatment variable was generally small, ranging between 1% and 4%. By including consideration of the significant interactive terms, the beneficiaries of these effects can be identified. Almost universally, the benefits of Atole were most evident in children from families at the lowest levels of socioeconomic status. In addition, in several cases, the beneficial effects of the Atole were also selectively observed in children who reached the upper percentiles of grade attainment.

Fewer effects of treatment were observed on the information-processing tasks. Atole treatment resulted in faster and more efficient processing on the memory task in both the entire sample and the cohort of maximum exposure; the one significant interaction (treatment × SES on paired associates) was observed only in the entire sample. On the outcomes that were affected, treatment differences accounted for between 1% and 2% of the variance in performance.

Results of the hierarchical analyses also provide information regarding the other variables entered into the model and their associations with the outcome variables. Overall, the full models accounted for between 15% (RPM) and 55% (literacy) of the variance in psychoeducational test performance and between 2% and 10% of the variance in information-processing outcomes. In general, males outperformed females on both the psychoeducational tests (i.e., reading, numeracy, and RPM) and the information-processing tasks (i.e., simple and choice reaction time, memory impulsivity, and percentage negative correct). Age was positively associated with performance on almost all the psychoeducational tests but not with performance on the information-processing tasks. Similarly, socioeconomic status and schooling were related to performance on most tests, but these associations were stronger for the psychoeducational than for the information-processing tasks. As indicated also by the correlational analyses, earlier school entry and attainment of a higher maximum grade were associated with improved test performance.

Cohort of Late Exposure

As noted at the beginning of this chapter, a cohort of subjects identified as having been exposed to the treatment only after 24 months of age was analyzed separately to test for the effects of early versus late exposure to treatment. After controlling for all other variables, treatment yielded two main effects: Atole subjects in this cohort performed significantly better on tests of numeracy and knowledge than Fresco subjects. As observed in the other analyses, there was also a significant treatment × grade interaction on the reading achievement test.

TABLE 21

Results of Hierarchical Regression Analyses for the Cohort of Maximum
Exposure on the Information-Processing Tests

Step and Variables	R^2	Model F	F to enter	Parameter Estimate	Direction of Effect Favors:
Simple reaction time:					
1. Sex	.01	1.67	4.54*	.018	Males
Age			.09	.001	...
Attendance[a]			.37	−.003	...
2. SES	.02	1.68	1.72	.003	...
3. Age at entry	.03	2.02	3.58	−.012	...
Max grade			1.73	−.007	...
4. Treatment (Rx)	.03	1.73	.03	−.002	...
Choice reaction time:					
1. Sex	.01	1.30	3.65*	.027	Males
Age			.08	.001	...
Attendance[a]			.17	.003	...
2. SES	.01	1.31	1.34	−.004	...
3. Age at entry	.02	1.04	.12	−.001	...
Max grade			.91	−.088	...
4. Treatment (Rx)	.02	1.04	1.01	−.016	...
Paired associates trials to criterion:					
1. Sex	.01	.72	.40	−.450	...
Age			.02	−.713	...
Attendance[a]			1.73	.538	...
2. SES	.01	.86	1.29	−.208	...
3. Age at entry	.05	3.15**	7.37**	.485	Younger
Max grade			7.98**	−1.210	Higher
4. Treatment (Rx)	.06	3.24**	3.65*	−1.476	Atole
Memory reaction time:					
1. Sex	.002	.24	.03	−.018	...
Age			.00	−.051	...
Attendance[a]			.69	.046	...
2. SES	.004	.43	1.01	−.024	...
3. Age at entry	.02	1.51	3.03	.037	...
Max grade			4.25*	−.117	Higher
4. Treatment (Rx)	.04	2.64**	9.25**	−.321	Higher
Impulsivity on memory task:					
1. Sex	.03	3.47*	4.88*	.285	Males
Age			.01	.176	...
Attendance[a]			5.52*	−.174	Higher
2. SES	.03	2.97*	1.44	−.039	Higher
3. Age at entry	.03	2.15*	1.03	.065	Younger
Max grade			.05	−.017	Higher
4. Treatment (Rx)	.04	2.14*	2.06	.208	Higher
% negative correct on memory task:					
1. Sex	.03	4.82**	10.26***	−.074	Males
Age			.02	−.038	...
Attendance[a]			4.17*	.027	Higher
2. SES	.05	4.84***	4.78*	.013	Higher

TABLE 21 (*Continued*)

Step and Variables	R^2	Model F	F to enter	Parameter Estimate	Direction of Effects Favors:
% negative correct on memory task:					
3. Age at entry	.07	5.19***	7.67**	−.023	Younger
Max grade			3.66	.026	. . .
4. Treatment (Rx)	.07	4.59***	1.02	.026	. . .
Efficiency on memory task:					
1. Sex	.01	1.50	3.35	.251	. . .
Age			.01	.076	. . .
Attendance[a]			1.13	−.085	. . .
2. SES	.03	2.74*	6.43**	−.088	Higher
3. Age at entry	.08	5.54***	11.93	.139	. . .
Max grade			9.80	−.248	. . .
4. Treatment (Rx)	.10	6.04***	8.40**	−.428	Atole

NOTE.—Sample sizes for the cohort of maximum exposure range from 335 to 416.

[a] Attendance is the residual value after regressing attendance on consumption.

* $p < .05$.　　　　*** $p < .001$.

** $p < .01$.

Although the pattern of findings was similar to that of the cohort of maximum exposure, the number and magnitude of significant findings were greatly reduced. The results from these analyses do not provide sufficient evidence for specifying the role of timing of the intervention.

EFFECTS OF TREATMENT ON NONSCHOOLED SUBJECTS

Unschooled subjects—that is, those for whom no schooling records were available and who were illiterate—were excluded from the main effects analyses and were analyzed separately, controlling only for socioeconomic differences and treatment × SES interactions.

Regressions were calculated for three of the psychoeducational tests (excluding literacy, reading, and the two Interamerican achievement tests since these required literacy skills) and the seven information-processing tasks. None of these analyses yielded a main effect of treatment at conventional levels of statistical significance or significant interactive terms.

As a result of the strict criteria imposed to define this group, sample sizes were quite small (ranging from 53 to 82). Power calculations for these analyses indicate relatively low power (around 58) for an effect size of .25 (Cohen, 1988), thus imposing a restriction on the interpretation of these results. Therefore, although no effects of Atole were observed within this restricted group, issues of low power preclude us from making definitive statements regarding the absence of effects in the unschooled sample.

VII. DISCUSSION

In the first section of this chapter, we review the issues that were discussed in Chapters III and IV, with a particular focus on whether the differences in the cognitive functioning of the Atole and the Fresco groups are best explained by the difference in the nutritional history of the subjects. The second section is devoted to a discussion of the results of the analyses of the psychoeducational and information-processing data. We then present a theoretical interpretation of the findings and, finally, consider their programmatic implications.

THE POWER OF A NUTRITIONAL EXPLANATION

The assessment of effects with which we are concerned was framed within a quasi-experimental design. As such, the study faces most, if not all, of the well-known risks involved in this type of experimental approach that we listed in our earlier discussion (see Chap. IV). In this case, the villages, but not the individuals, were randomized into one of the two nutritional treatments. One might argue that utilizing this randomization would allow for a more powerful analytic strategy than electing to use the individual as the unit of analysis: theoretically, the four villages could have functioned as the units for analysis. However, in our view, the benefits of such a strategy would be illusory; the analysis would be legitimate only if the design had been that of a true experiment and included randomization as well as blinding of both subject and personnel. The intervention study failed to meet both these criteria. From our own analyses, we now know that randomization did not render the Atole and the Fresco villages comparable on all possible confounding variables, and neither subjects nor field personnel were blinded with regard to treatment.

Our analyses of the follow-up data established long-term developmental effects of nutritional supplementation, particularly among those at the lower end of the social and economic distribution in the villages. To our knowledge, no previous study has tested the effects of supplementary feeding during the first years of life on intellectual functioning assessed 10–15 years later. Our results are the first of this kind to be reported, and most readers of the nutrition-behavior literature will find them unexpected (Pollitt, 1988). However, it is necessary to review alternative explanations before an inference of a nutrition effect can be drawn.

In Chapter IV, we discussed the foremost threats to the validity of the conclusion that we propose; the most important among them were the nonequivalence between villages (both during the intervention and in the 10-year interval between the longitudinal and the follow-up study) with regard to factors capable of affecting the outcomes of concern, differences in the delivery and consumption of Atole and Fresco related to the differing nutritional properties of the two drinks, and the different patterns of attendance at the feeding stations where each of the supplements was administered. Although we lack the necessary information to reject them completely, our analyses of the available data converge to indicate that none of these alternatives can completely account for the differences in the cognitive functioning of subjects from Atole and from Fresco villages: the internal validity of the nutritional explanation is not compromised by these challenges.

In addition to ruling out alternative explanations, we have also established that a nutrition experiment did in fact take place and that the nutritional differences between the Atole and the Fresco villages had demonstrable developmental implications. The differences in the composition and the actual consumption of the two supplements suggest that the individuals who received the Atole were better nourished, particularly since Atole consumption truly supplemented the diet rather than merely substituting for other foods (see, e.g., Chap. IV).

Although the presence of a nutritional treatment is unquestionable, we cannot test the original protein hypothesis, nor can we specify which nutrient(s) determined the observed differences in outcomes. We do know that the two supplements were equivalent in micronutrients per unit of volume; however, the actual consumption of the Atole and Fresco supplements differed. Thus, when actual micronutrient consumption data were analyzed in terms of recommended dietary allowances (National Research Council, 1989), there was no equivalence between the two groups in that regard. Because the subjects in the Atole group consistently consumed more micronutrients than the subjects in the Fresco villages in the postnatal period, we cannot rule out the possibility that factors such as iron contributed to the test differences between groups (Pollitt, in press).

Finally, we must consider whether our nutritional explanation conforms with the current understanding of the nature and determinants of human development. We argued in Chapter III that both theory and data support the possibility of effects of early supplementary feeding on cognitive development in adolescence. Early supplementary feeding of nutritionally at-risk infants and preschool children results in a developmental advantage and is likely to have beneficial long-term effects, just as the provision of educational opportunities to young children living in poverty has been shown to have beneficial long-term effects on their social behavior.

In addition, longitudinal studies of children exposed to stress factors suggest that, while single events are generally not a sufficient condition to affect development, the probability of deviancy increases when multiple stress factors coexist or interact in synergistic fashion. We have found that those children who were at the lowest levels of the SES distribution and received Fresco performed less well on the battery of psychoeducational tests than any of the other groups of children.

In contrast to the strong evidence on the effects of Atole observed among the subjects in the cohort of maximum exposure, the range of supplement effects on the subjects with late exposure (after 2 years of age) was narrower. There were main effects of Atole on the knowledge and numeracy tests and a significant interaction between treatment and grade attained on reading achievement, similar to those found in the cohort of maximum exposure.

This difference in the range of effects observed among the two groups suggests that the behavioral development of children is more sensitive to nutritional factors during the first years of life, particularly during the period of rapid growth in the brain and body. However, the effects on this late exposure cohort show that, in a nutritionally at-risk population, dietary improvements after the second year of life, following the peak period of growth and change, will still have long-term developmental benefits.

In sum, the evaluations of competing explanations suggest that the dietary experimental intervention is the most likely determinant of the observed differences in test performance.

REFLECTIONS ON PARTICULAR FINDINGS

The findings that we have reported are most prominent in the cohort of maximum exposure. Thus, unless otherwise specified, the discussion that follows focuses on this group.

The coherence of the results summarized at the close of Chapter VI is perhaps their most striking feature. Among them, the most conspicuous is the significant interactive effects·of treatment × SES on five of the seven tests (except reading and literacy) included in the psychoeducational test battery. Consistently, the subjects who benefited the most from the Atole were those at the lowest levels of the SES continuum. A second major finding is the interactive effect of treatment × grade: those who had reached the highest grades in school and had received the Atole fared better than all other groups on all three tests tapping reading skills. In the information-processing test battery, there were main effects on memory and paired associates tasks; none of the interactive terms were significant.

The breadth of effects was coupled with their modest size. The maximum R^2 accounted for by the Atole treatment was 5% (e.g., on the vocabulary test). On some tests, although maximum R^2 was statistically significant, it represented only about 1% of the variance (e.g., numeracy). However, because these modest effects were generalized over a wide range of mental abilities, they are likely to have resulted in significant differences between the behavioral repertoire of the subjects in the Atole and the Fresco villages. The coherence of these findings extends back, at least in part, to the earlier longitudinal study. At 4 and 5 years of age, the interactive term treatment × SES accounted for significant portions of the variance in the cognitive Factor 1 (derived from the battery of tests administered during the preschool period). As is the case in adolescence, the subjects who benefited the most from the early supplementary feeding were those at the lower end of the SES distribution within the Atole group. Thus, the activation of the processes that resulted in the developmental advantage of the low-SES group must have occurred early in life.

In contrast to what was observed at 4 and 5 years of age, the findings at 3 and 6 years showed neither main nor interactive effects. The absence of effects at 3 years of age agrees with the theoretical model that we propose below, one that incorporates the notion that the probabilities of detecting effects increase as the child grows older. Recall that the effects of treatment during the first 2 years of age on the Composite Infant Scale were restricted to the motor scale at 24 months of age.

The lack of either interactive or main effects at age 6 is not an aesthetically pleasing finding and cannot readily be explained. The personal characteristics and history of the subjects who were included in the statistical tests run for this age group do not differ in any substantive way from those subjects who were assessed at 4 and 5 years of age. The data do not offer any suggestive evidence to explain the finding.

In many respects, the subjects at the lower end of the SES distributions who benefited from the Atole in adolescence were disadvantaged compared to the rest of their community. For instance, on average, the mothers of these children had no more than 1 year of elementary schooling. The fathers had the lowest levels of occupation, and their housing was of the poorest quality across villages (e.g., small, without toilets, thatched roofs). During their preschool years, these subjects performed poorly on the cognitive test battery, and they were also shorter and lighter than other children of the same age.

The rate of physical growth, performance on preschool tests, and SES background of the low-SES subjects who benefited from the Atole suggest that their early development had been at high risk both in absolute terms and also by the standards of their own community. This high risk, moreover, was not derived solely from poor nutrition; it also stemmed from the many other adverse conditions of their environment (e.g., poverty and disease). An assessment of risk during these subjects' early formative years would probably have predicted poor test performance during adolescence. Yet their test performance in the follow-up was comparable to that of subjects at the highest SES level, and it was better than that of a comparable SES group in the Fresco villages.

The protective effect of the Atole conforms with results from longitudinal studies of exposure to early biological (e.g., low birth weight) and SES stress factors in which characteristics of the caregiving environment appear to shield the development of children against the adverse effects of exposure to such risk factors. For example, in a study of children in Kauai (Werner, 1986), the availability of alternate caregivers, the mother's work load (e.g., steady employment outside the household), and the amount of attention given to the children by the primary caregiver proved to be factors that protected the development of children considered to be at high risk in early life.

The significant interactions between treatment and maximum grade attained on outcomes such as the achievement tests suggest that the effects of the Atole were also modified by particular characteristics of the subjects. Recall that the relation between maximum grade attained and the Interamerican reading and vocabulary scores was positive for Atole but not Fresco subjects; Atole children who were in the upper percentiles of grade attainment scored significantly higher than Fresco children.

Intuitively, the interactions between treatment and grade seem to conflict with the interactions between treatment and SES, where those who were worse off were more likely to benefit from the dietary treatment. However, in the context of a rural society living in poverty, the differences in the developmental implications of SES and of maximum grade attained resolve such an apparent discrepancy. SES is a carrier variable of family conditions that were relatively stable over the lifetime of the subjects in the study and that, even among the families who were better off, pointed to a state of unmet basic human needs. On the other hand, maximum grade attained reflects increased exposure to a favorable environment as the children broaden their educational opportunities from one year to the next. This distinction in the developmental meaning of SES and maximum grade attained explains, as discussed below, why those at the lowest end of the SES distribution and those with the highest levels of formal education benefited most from Atole.

Further light on the developmental significance of the two sets of inter-actions that we have discussed is shed by a consideration of the three-way interaction that emerged in the analysis of the reading achievement test. As noted, the SES × grade interaction was significant for the Fresco but not for the Atole villages. Within the Fresco villages, associations between SES and achievement were positive and significant for both low and high levels of grade attainment. Conversely, these associations were not significant in the case of Atole.

Such a differential pattern in the interactions suggests that the truism that SES affects cognitive test performance is fulfilled in the Fresco group, independent of whether the focus is on opposite sides of the distribution of maximum grade attained. This is not the case with Atole: the truism is challenged since SES has no effect on test scores at either extreme of the school grade distribution—in order words, the high nutrient supplement is acting as a social equalizer.

A THEORETICAL INTERPRETATION

We now sketch a theoretical model of the linkage that we propose between early nutrition and later development. We recognize that these efforts could be similar to painting broad strokes over a large canvas, repre-senting a reality that may well be far too complex to be tested experimen-tally. The model is first discussed in general terms, followed by a description of its relevance to the particular findings from the follow-up.

The model builds on well-grounded empirical information that, among nutritionally at-risk children, variations in nutrition status (i.e., protein, en-ergy, and micronutrient deficiencies such as iron and zinc) account for sig-nificant variations in physical growth, motor maturation, and physical activ-ity (Husaini et al., 1991; Martorell & Habicht, 1986; Meeks Gardner, Grantham-McGregor, Chang, & Powell, 1990; Rutishauser & Whitehead, 1972; Simonson, Sherwin, Anilane, Yu, & Chow, 1969; Super, Herrera, & Mora, 1990; Vasquez-Velasquez, 1988). In Guatemala, the children in the Atole villages were taller and heavier than those in the Fresco villages, and such differences continued into adolescence (Martorell et al., 1980; Martorell, Rivera, & Kaplowitz, 1990). They were also motorically more mature at 24 months than the children in the Fresco group. Because motor activity was not assessed in the study, we do not know whether the children in the two groups differed in this regard; however, it is likely that this was the case. Both theory and empirical studies suggest that one of the mecha-nisms available to maintain energy balance among malnourished children is a reduction of energy expenditure in motor activity (Beaton, 1984; Grantham-McGregor, Meeks Gardner, Walker, & Powell, 1990).

We conjecture that the effects of malnutrition on body size, motor maturation, and physical activity are the linkages between malnutrition and delays in behavioral development over time. In particular, we conjecture that small body size, delays in motor maturation, and reduced physical activity contribute to the gradual formation of styles or modalities of social-emotional and behavioral interactions between the malnourished child and the environment that slow cognitive development and educational progress. This proposition is an outgrowth of current theorizing that the associations between particular biological characteristics of children and their environment tend to covary with each other (Plomin, DeFries, & Loehlin, 1977; Wachs & Plomin, 1991). The following is a more detailed analysis of our theoretical proposal.

1. In both industrialized and preindustrial societies, accelerated physical growth and height are associated with comparatively better performance on developmental scales in early childhood and intelligence and school achievement tests in adolescence. While the exact mechanisms behind these associations remain unclear and are likely to differ from one society to another, one possible explanation is that physical growth and body size determine in part ways children are cared for and treated socially. In particular, small children are likely to be treated as younger than their chronological age, and they trigger caretaking behaviors of nurturance and protection at a time when children of a similar age but of average size and maturity are searching for autonomy and independence from their caretakers. The opposite will be true for comparatively larger, more mature-looking children; their physical attributes will induce caretaking behaviors that, on average, are reserved for older children. For example, the mothers of malnourished children maintain more frequent physical contact and closer proximity to their offspring than mothers of well-nourished children of the same age (Graves, 1976, 1978; Lozoff, 1988; Lozoff, Klein, & Prabucki, 1986). Similar patterns of behavioral interactions between caretaker and offspring are also observed in animals; in some species, the frequency of adult-offspring contact correlates negatively with the offspring's age and size (Harper, 1970; Konner, 1976; Moss, 1967; Trivers, 1974).

2. It is now well established that malnutrition delays motor maturation in infants and young children. In keeping with the first proposition, there is also evidence that the timetable of motor maturation influences the nature and range of contacts that the organism has with its physical and social environment. Motor milestones, particularly those of self-locomotion (i.e., crawling, creeping, and walking), transform the child's perception of and physical relations with the physical space and the elements within it (Bertenthal & Campos, 1990; Bremner & Bryant, 1985). These developmental changes lead, in turn, to the acquisition of new perceptual skills (e.g., depth perception). In addition, self-directed locomotion increases social contacts,

broadens social experiences, and enhances affective contacts with adults (Gustafson, 1984). Of concern to us here is that, because of delays in motor maturation, malnutrition limits the opportunities that these children have to move about the environment, learn from it, and develop cognitive skills that children who are of a similar age, but more mature, are acquiring.

3. Our last proposition is that physical activity in children is positively related to exploratory behavior—behavior exploring the physical and social environment. We recognize that there is not much empirical evidence to support this proposition; however, the evidence that is available comes mostly from studies of well-nourished groups, where, under ordinary circumstances, the level of motor activity of children is independent of their nutrient intake. In these groups, the critical issues may be the child's capacity to self-regulate and to modulate activity according to the demands of the environment rather than the characteristic level of activity (Wachs, 1990).

We conjecture that there is a positive relation between physical activity and exploratory behavior in those situations where the motor activity of children is partly determined by the intake of energy and micronutrients (e.g., iron). This postulate stems from the notion that one of the mechanisms available to the organism to maintain energy balance is to reduce the expenditure of energy through a decrement of motor activity. Thus, under these circumstances, the average level of activity in children is lower than the level of activity they would display if their nutrient intake would meet their physiological requirements. This low average level of activity is what we believe is associated with the reduced amount of exploration of the environment evinced among malnourished children.

The importance of exploratory behavior has been discussed at length in the developmental psychology literature (Berlyne, 1966; Bruner, 1968; Piaget, 1952). In fact, early exploration of events, people, and objects is seen as the foundation of cognition. With the development of perceptual systems and the maturation of new action systems, the young child discovers the particular attributes of each new physical and social stimulus that are relevant to the context and to his or her developmental stage (Gibson, 1988).

In sum, we propose that the effects of malnutrition on body size, motor maturation, and physical activity mediate the relation between malnutrition and delayed cognitive and behavioral development. In particular, there are three basic propositions: (1) Children who are small because of their nutritional history induce caretaking behaviors and social responses from others that are generally reserved for children of a comparatively younger age. (2) Their slow motor maturation delays the acquisition of particular cognitive abilities and social behaviors. (3) Their low level of motor activity that results from the need to maintain energy balance limits the exploration of the physical and social environment. These three sets of effects are not limited to a particular age; they operate and express themselves throughout the child's early, middle, and late childhood and adolescence. They activate mechanisms that span years in the lives of children who live under social, economic, and physical circumstances that are similar to those in rural Guatemala. The final outcome is the attainment of a level of cognitive competence that is behind the level of other children and adolescents of the same chronological age with a history of having received adequate nutrition.

The definition of effects that we propose is substantively different from that which assumes that malnutrition has direct effects on the central nervous system and, therefore, on cognitive function. However, we do not deny that such direct effects might indeed exist; the two explanatory models are not mutually exclusive. At issue now is to fit the model to the data that show no main effects on the psychoeducational tests but do show significant interactions: in one case, between treatment and SES and, in the second, between treatment and maximum grade attained.

Within the context of a poor rural society in Guatemala, the families with the lowest economic and social resources must face the most severe constraints to meet the health (e.g., medical care, hygiene, and sanitation), nutrition (e.g., dietary quality), and developmental (e.g., educational opportunities) needs of their children. This was also the case among the severely impoverished families who benefited the most from the Atole; in such a context, the Atole compensated in part for the existing constraints and pushed the children in the study toward faster growth and healthier development. In particular, their comparatively larger size, earlier motor maturation, better health, and, possibly, increased exploratory activities must have induced particular caretaking and social responses and led to the development of behaviors and the early acquisition of cognitive skills that compensated somewhat for the severe limitations of their impoverished households, which failed to meet their developmental needs. On the other hand, these effects did not occur at the other end of the SES distribution because, within the limits of a poor, rural community, even in the family and household environment of those who were better off there is not much that can be offered to a healthy child. In other words, there is a ceiling in the provision of potential benefits given to the children in the context of rural family poverty.

A natural extension of this argument is that, if the children who received Atole would have been exposed to an environment without such a ceiling, then the benefit of the nutritional supplement would have been greater. This postulated incremental effect is what we think explains the significant interaction between treatment and maximum grade attained. Despite all their limitations (Gorman & Pollitt, 1992), the schools in the villages made possible the effects of the Atole because they provided opportunities for intellectual growth. Accordingly, the higher the grade attained—that is, the greater the exposure to schooling—the greater the effects of the nutritional supplement.

The explanatory model also accounts for the effects observed among the children included in the late exposure cohort because nutritional supplementation accelerates growth velocity even after the second year of life, albeit at a lower rate than what is observed when it is implemented before the second year. Modest physical and health advantages among those in the late exposure cohort who received Atole are likely to have activated the same process that we have described in connection with the children in the maximum exposure cohort. The difference between the advantages of the two cohorts is a matter of degree of effects.

An empirical test of the model that we propose is not feasible because we lack the necessary data concerning motor development milestones and physical activity measurements; moreover, even if these data were available, the samples would become too small to permit analysis once all the relevant variables were taken into consideration. At this stage, this model remains strictly conjectural.

POLICY IMPLICATIONS

The provision of health and nutrition services is a means of promoting growth and development among children. In the United States, for example, although the specific objectives of food assistance programs are often not clearly defined, some programs (like the federally funded Special Supplemental Food Program for Women, Infants, and Children [WIC]) target nutritionally at-risk groups in order to prevent growth and developmental delays associated with malnutrition (Pollitt, Garza, & Leibel, 1984; Rush et al., 1988). Do the results of the Guatemala study provide a public health justification for food assistance programs such as WIC? In particular, do the data support a claim that such programs will help prevent cognitive developmental delays? Such preventive effects would have broader social and economic implications if it were to be shown that these kinds of delays affect work capacity and productivity.

The findings that we report support the assertion that, among nutritionally at-risk infants and children, early supplementary feeding contributes to a salutary development of the complex mental abilities required in an industrialized society among those at the lowest socioeconomic levels. However, they do not support a claim that the provision of food alone assures a significant net increase in daily intake. The Guatemala study was a major undertaking, with a solid and efficient administrative infrastructure created for research purposes. There was close access to the target group and continuous prompting to attend a station, where subjects received the supplement and socialized with other people. Without this prompting, the food supplement may not have had the desired effect. In their comprehensive review of supplementary feeding programs in developing countries, Beaton and Ghassemi (1982) concluded that the net increases in food intake were often lower than intended.

A related issue regarding treatment effects and their programmatic implications is the nutritional status of the target population. The prevalence of growth retardation in the population studied in Guatemala points to a high risk of malnutrition among infants and children. For example, a recent analysis of anthropometric data of subjects who had been measured at 3 years of age showed that 25.8% of the sample had severe stunting (3 standard deviations or more below the reference median) and that 42.5% had moderate stunting (2.9–2.0 standard deviations below the median) (Martorell, Rivera, Kaplowitz, & Pollitt, 1991). These estimates are similar to those made prior to the initiation of the longitudinal study in 1969 (Martorell, Habicht, & Klein, 1982).

The external validity of the Guatemala findings must be assessed in context, and generalizations are restricted to populations with a nutritional status similar to that in the rural villages in Guatemala. Moreover, the interactions between the nutritional treatment and SES indicate that, even within these populations, there is a differential response to treatment. Not all those in a nutritionally at-risk population benefited from the intervention.

On the surface, it may appear that findings of SES × treatment interactions speak clearly in favor of targeting treatment to individuals of lower SES. However, a closer look shows that the problem is more complex. The interaction between treatment and maximum grade attained indicates that individuals who may already have some social and educational advantages may be helped to excel even further by nutritional supplementation. Programmatically, it may be easiest to identify and target only those at the lowest end of the SES distribution within a community, but doing so means that other children who could benefit from the supplement will not receive it.

From a policy perspective, it must be recognized that the social or economic significance of the psychological test findings obtained in the Guatemala study is not readily apparent. While the construct validity of the tests was supported on theoretical grounds, no assessment was made of their predictive validity with reference to a behavioral criterion such as social adjustment or work productivity. The wide age range in the sample precluded such an assessment since many subjects were still in school and not earning any income. Moreover, to our knowledge, there is no relevant information from comparable rural populations in Latin America that could be used to establish the ecological significance of the Guatemala findings. Thus, the test score differences cannot be translated into other, more tangible terms, such as work productivity, earnings, or social adjustment. Although it is theoretically justified to assume that variation in scores on tests of reading and numerical ability are associated with variations in social and economic behaviors, it is also conceivable that such covariations may be lower than expected in a society in which basic human needs remain unmet.

The effects of public health programs, particularly behavioral effects, need to be analyzed in the context of a society's explicit and implicit social policy. In the context of rural Guatemala, the benefits of a supplementary program in enhancing development must be contrasted with the consequences of other existing conditions that counter such development. The school system, for example, is terribly inefficient and does not respond to the basic educational needs of the population (Gorman & Pollitt, 1992). Less than half the children enrolled in the first grade finish primary school, and many remain functionally illiterate. It is highly unlikely that the provision of food will prevent or remedy the consequences of not receiving an adequate formal education in a changing society.

Programmatic actions that focus on unmet nutritional needs and that have beneficial effects on human cognitive development are potentially a step forward in social policy. However, in our view, such actions are deceptive if they are framed in the context of a social policy that disregards other basic human needs and does not attend to the overall quality of life. Unmet nutritional needs generally coexist with, among other things, unmet needs in education, housing, sanitation, and health care. Only by meeting all these needs in conjunction with nutritional needs will we have truly moved forward toward a fair, humane society that sustains the rights of children and fosters cognitive and social-emotional development.

AVERAGE NUTRIENT INTAKES
OF ATOLE AND FRESCO SUBJECTS

TABLE A1

MEANS AND STANDARD DEVIATIONS OF SUPPLEMENT INTAKES: ENTIRE SAMPLE

Period of Supplementation	Atole Male (N)	Atole Female (N)	Fresco Male (N)	Fresco Female (N)
Prenatal:				
Kcal	106.5 ± 95.1	99.0 ± 89.3	85.6 ± 72.2	75.8 ± 61.9
Protein (g)	7.5 ± 6.7	7.0 ± 6.3	0	0
	(260)	(235)	(191)	(164)
Lactation:				
0–12 months:				
Kcal	91.2 ± 145.0	77.3 ± 127.2	36.0 ± 52.8	32.2 ± 53.6
Protein (g)	6.4 ± 10.2	5.4 ± 9.0	0	0
	(665)	(642)	(462)	(433)
12–24 months:				
Kcal	61.5 ± 106.8	55.6 ± 93.7	40.8 ± 57.1	38.6 ± 61.9
Protein (g)	4.3 ± 7.5	4.0 ± 6.6	0	0
	(609)	(576)	(411)	(395)
0–24 months:				
Kcal	73.8 ± 117.7	63.6 ± 101.8	36.2 ± 49.7	33.7 ± 52.5
Protein (g)	5.2 ± 8.3	4.5 ± 7.2	0	0
	(665)	(642)	(462)	(433)
Postnatal:				
0–12 months:				
Kcal	36.1 ± 64.9	27.0 ± 53.2	2.8 ± 5.2	2.4 ± 5.1
Protein (g)	2.5 ± 4.6	1.9 ± 3.8	0	0
	(665)	(642)	(462)	(433)
12–24 months:				
Kcal	60.9 ± 92.1	55.2 ± 85.4	11.2 ± 16.2	8.5 ± 12.9
Protein (g)	4.3 ± 6.5	3.8 ± 6.0	0	0
	(609)	(576)	(411)	(395)
24–36 months:				
Kcal	78.7 ± 108.5	76.1 ± 107.7	24.8 ± 31.7	18.9 ± 24.3
Protein (g)	5.4 ± 7.7	5.3 ± 7.6	0	0
	(551)	(527)	(372)	(359)

TABLE A2

Means and Standard Deviations of Supplement Intakes: Maximum Exposure

Period of Supplementation	Atole Male (N)	Atole Female (N)	Fresco Male (N)	Fresco Female (N)
Prenatal:				
Kcal	120.3 ± 98.3	101.0 ± 82.3	84.8 ± 65.9	70.8 ± 60.5
Protein (g)	8.5 ± 6.9	7.1 ± 5.8	0	0
	(148)	(134)	(126)	(103)
Lactation:				
0–12 months:				
Kcal	171.6 ± 166.7	149.7 ± 148.5	54.4 ± 57.8	46.4 ± 53.2
Protein (g)	12.1 ± 11.8	10.6 ± 10.5	0	0
	(192)	(175)	(172)	(142)
12–24 months:				
Kcal	112.2 ± 131.2	109.6 ± 115.6	64.4 ± 61.5	56.6 ± 62.8
Protein (g)	7.9 ± 9.3	7.7 ± 8.2	0	0
	(188)	(173)	(172)	(141)
0–24 months:				
Kcal	140.8 ± 142.0	129.0 ± 124.7	59.4 ± 54.6	51.3 ± 54.4
Protein (g)	9.9 ± 10.0	9.8 ± 8.8	0	0
	(192)	(175)	(172)	(142)
Postnatal:				
0–12 months:				
Kcal	69.4 ± 80.6	54.7 ± 65.6	4.0 ± 6.3	3.0 ± 4.5
Protein (g)	4.9 ± 5.7	3.9 ± 4.6	0	0
	(192)	(175)	(172)	(142)
12–24 months:				
Kcal	112.8 ± 108.6	108.3 ± 94.9	15.9 ± 17.7	11.7 ± 12.9
Protein (g)	8.0 ± 7.7	7.6 ± 6.7	0	0
	(188)	(173)	(172)	(141)
24–36 months:				
Kcal	137.9 ± 121.7	144.7 ± 125.1	31.2 ± 32.3	27.5 ± 24.7
Protein (g)	9.7 ± 8.6	10.2 ± 8.8	0	0
	(188)	(172)	(171)	(140)

DESCRIPTIONS OF TESTS USED IN THE ANALYSIS OF THE PRESCHOOL BATTERY

Embedded Figures.—This test assesses children's ability to distinguish a figure from among a meaningful visual array. It was developed by Witkin, Dyk, Faterson, Goodenough, and Karp (1962) as a measure of the tendency to be field dependent (influenced by the context) or field independent. There were two versions of the test. In the 3-year-old version, the child was first shown a picture of a common figure, then a larger picture with that figure embedded in it, and asked to point to the figure. The first nine items required the child to select the target figure from a group of other forms, and the second nine required the child to locate the embedded figure. The version administered to 4–7-year-olds used a red triangle as the target figure. After practice, a copy of the triangle remained visible to the child, who was asked to find where it was hidden in each of 12 pictures. The score was the number of items located correctly.

Memory for Digits.—This test is similar to those included in the Stanford-Binet and the WISC. The child was asked to repeat sequences of numbers read by the tester at a rate of two per sec. The lowest number of digits per span was two, and there were four series at each length of span. The score was the total number of digits recalled correctly, plus one point for each span totally correct.

Memory for Sentences.—The child was asked to repeat meaningful sentences after the examiner, who read them at a rate of two words per sec. The items were a series of sentences of differing length, with 2 items at each length (number of words); all words were two syllables long. The score was the total number of words correctly recalled, plus one point for a correct sentence.

Vocabulary Naming and Recognition.—This was a picture vocabulary test, similar to the early items of the Peabody Picture Vocabulary Test. None of the items in this test required inferences about actions. The child was shown a notebook containing about four pictures per page, all of which depicted objects common in the village. The child was first asked to name each picture; various synonyms were acceptable. The total number correct was the *Naming* score. After seeing all the pictures, the name of each picture that had not been named or had been named incorrectly was supplied, and the child was asked to point to the appropriate picture. The *Recognition* score was the total number of items named, plus the number recognized.

Draw-a-Line Slowly.—This test was developed by Maccoby, Dowley, Hagen, and Degerman (1965) to measure impulse control. As reported by the authors, this measure was significantly associated with Stanford-Binet scores in a preschool population but was unrelated to overall activity level measured by "actometers"; it may measure ability to follow instructions as well as impulse control. The child was asked to draw a line between two marks on a page as fast as possible and then to do it as slowly as possible. The score was derived from the latter; it represents the velocity of the line, that is, its length divided by the time taken to draw it. A lower score indicated greater impulse control.

Persistence on a Puzzle.—This test attempted to measure persistence in an impossible situation. The child was given a puzzle with 18 pieces, which he or she was supposed to fit into the board; in reality, this could not be accomplished by any means. The child was given a maximum of 3 min to work on the puzzle. The score was the number of 10-sec intervals that the child continued to work on the puzzle.

Memory for Objects.—This test was both a standard memory test and a measure of a child's ability to use categories of objects in order to enhance recall. The children were shown a large round circular tablet with 12 familiar objects placed around the edge of the circle. These items belonged to three conceptual categories (animals, clothing, and kitchen utensils). The children were asked to look at the objects; the objects were then covered with a cloth, and the child was asked to recall as many as possible. The score was the number of objects recalled.

Verbal Inferences.—This test was a Guatemalan adaptation of a verbal analogies test used in both the Stanford-Binet and the WISC. The child was first given two simple test items; corrections were given if the child could not complete the item or completed it incorrectly. A partial sentence was read to the child, who was expected to complete the idea by supplying the missing word. The first two examples were the following: "Shoes go on feet; a hat goes on ———"; and, "Water is to drink, tortillas are to ———." If the child did not understand these first two, the test was not administered.

Knox Cubes, Slow Version.—This test was an adaptation of the Leiter (1940) International Performance Scale. The child was asked to repeat a series of taps on four stimuli. A board with four small familiar miniature objects (fan, bow, etc.) lined up in a row was shown to the child. With a stick the length of a pencil, the tester tapped these objects in a particular order; the child was then asked to tap them in the same order. The slow presentation had 1 tap per sec (the subsequent fast presentation with 4 taps per sec was not used). The score was the number of series of taps correctly completed.

Incomplete Figures.—Both the Stanford-Binet and the WPSSI contain a measure of the child's ability to identify a missing part of a common object in a picture. The child was shown 16 items common to Guatemalan village life and asked to point to where the missing part should be. The score was the total number of missing parts correctly identified.

Elimination of the Odd Figure.—The child was shown a series of five drawings in a row and was asked to point to the one that was different. Some differed on perceptual grounds (e.g., a girl with black rather than white shoes) and some on conceptual grounds (e.g., one child in the picture was doing a different kind of activity from the other children). The score was the total number of items correctly identified.

Block Design.—This test was similar to one of the subtests of the WPSSI. The child was asked to replicate a design displayed on a card by using a series of small blocks. Some of the more difficult designs use blocks with diagonal lines. The score was based on points for each correct cube's color, position, and orientation, plus one point for a completely correct design.

Memory for Designs.—This test was designed to assess children's ability to remember a design and replicate it using 1-inch cubic blocks, painted a different color on each side. The examiner constructed a design using four colored blocks (red, green, yellow, and blue, plus some blocks with diagonals) and allowed the child to inspect it for 5 sec. The blocks were then scrambled, and the child was asked to reconstruct the design from memory. Three trials were allowed per design. The first two items had only two blocks. The score was the number of points based on the color and the position of the blocks.

REFERENCES

Adair, L. S., & Pollitt, E. (1985). Outcome of maternal nutritional supplementation: A comprehensive review of the Bacon Chow study. *American Journal of Clinical Nutrition,* **41,** 948–978.

Arnold, R. D. (1969). Reliability of test scores for the young "bilingual" disadvantaged. *Reading Teacher,* **22**(4), 341–345.

Autret, M., & Béhar, M. (1954). Le syndrome de polycarence de l'enfance en Amerique centrale (kwashiorkor) [The syndrome of multiple deficiencies in children of Central America (kwashiorkor)]. *Bulletin of the World Health Organization,* **11,** 891–966.

Balderston, J. B. (1981). Determinants of children's school participation. In J. B. Balderston, A. B. Wilson, M. E. Freire, & M. S. Simonen (Eds.), *Malnourished children of the rural poor.* Boston: Auburn.

Barahini, M. N. (1973). Preliminary norms on Raven's Progressive Matrices as applied to Iranian children. *Educational and Psychological Measurement,* **34,** 983–988.

Barrett, D. E., Radke-Yarrow, M., & Klein, R. E. (1983). Chronic malnutrition and child behavior: Effects of early caloric supplementation on social and emotional functioning at school age. In S. Chess & A. Thomas (Eds.), *Annual progress in child psychiatry and child development.* New York: Brunner/Mazel.

Bayley, N. (1969). *Manual for the Bayley Scales of infant development.* New York: Psychological Corp.

Beaton, G. H. (1984). Adaptation to and accommodation of long-term energy intake: A commentary on the Conference on Energy Intake and Activity. In E. Pollitt & P. Amante (Eds.), *Energy intake and activity.* New York: Alan R. Liss.

Beaton, G. H., & Ghassemi, H. (1982). Supplementary feeding programs for young children in developing countries. *American Journal of Clinical Nutrition,* **35**(4), 864–916.

Bengoa, J. M. (1974). The problem of malnutrition. *WHO Chronicle,* **28,** 3–7.

Berlyne, D. E. (1966). Curiosity and exploration. *Science,* **171,** 818–820.

Bernstein, B. (1961). Social class and linguistic development: A theory of social learning. In A. H. Hasely, J. Floud, & C. A. Anderson (Eds.), *Economy, education and society.* New York: Free Press.

Bertenthal, B. I., & Campos, J. J. (1990). A systems approach to the organizing effects of self-produced locomotion during infancy. In C. Rovee-Collier & L. P. Lipsitt (Eds.), *Advances in infancy research* (Vol. **6**). Norwood, NJ: Ablex.

Brazelton, T. B. (1973). *Neonatal assessment scale* (Clinics in Developmental Medicine, Vol. **50**). London: S.I.M.P./Heinemann.

Brazelton, T. B., Tronick, E., Lechtig, A., Lasky, R. E., & Klein, R. E. (1977). The behavior of nutritionally deprived Guatemalan infants. *Developmental Medicine and Child Neurology,* **19,** 364–367.

Bremner, J. G., & Bryant, P. E. (1985). Active movement and development of spatial abilities in infancy. In H. M. Wellman (Ed.), *Children's searching: The development of search skill and spatial representation*. Hillsdale, NJ: Erlbaum.

Bronfenbrenner, U. (1968). Early deprivation in mammals: A cross-species analysis. In G. Newton & S. Levine (Eds.), *Early experience and behavior*. Springfield, IL: Charles C. Thomas.

Bronfenbrenner, U. (1974). *A report on longitudinal evaluations of preschool programs: Vol. 2. Is early intervention effective?* (DHEW Publication No. [OHD] 76-30025). Washington, DC: U.S. Department of Health, Education, and Welfare, Office of Human Development, Office of Child Development, Children's Bureau.

Bronfenbrenner, U. (1979). *The ecology of human development: Experiments by nature and design*. Cambridge, MA: Harvard University Press.

Bruner, J. S. (1968). *Processes of cognitive growth: Infancy* (Heinz Werner Lecture Series). Worcester, MA: Clark University Press.

Cabak, V., & Najdanvic, R. (1965). Effect of undernutrition in early life on physical and mental development. *Archives of Disease in Childhood, 40*, 532–534.

Campbell, D. T., & Stanley, J. C. (1963). *Experimental and quasi-experimental designs for research*. Chicago: Rand McNally.

Ceci, S. J. (1991). How much does schooling influence general intelligence and its cognitive components: A reassessment of the evidence. *Developmental Psychology, 27*(5), 703–722.

Cohen, J. (1988). *Statistical power analysis for the behavioral sciences* (2d ed.). Hillsdale, NJ: Erlbaum.

Consortium for Longitudinal Studies. (1983). *As the twig is bent . . . : Lasting effects of preschool programs*. Hillsdale, NJ: Erlbaum.

Cook, T. D., & Campbell, D. T. (1979). *Quasi-experimentation: Design and analysis issues for field settings*. Chicago: Rand McNally.

Cravioto, J., DeLicardie, E. R., & Birch, H. G. (1966). Nutrition, growth and neurointegrative development: An experimental and ecologic study. *Pediatrics, 38*(Suppl. 2, Pt. 2), 319–372.

Cravioto, J., & Robles, B. (1965). Evolution of adaptive and motor behavior during rehabilitation from kwashiorkor. *American Journal of Orthopsychiatry, 35*, 449–464.

Division of Human Development. (1977). *Section IA. of the write-up contract: Background of the INCAP study*. Guatemala City: Institute of Nutrition of Central America and Panama. Mimeo.

Division of Human Development. (n.d.). *Contract article I-A: Introductory description*. Guatemala City: Institute of Nutrition of Central America and Panama.

Engle, P. L., & Levin, R. J. (1984). Sex differences in the effects of malnutrition on mental development: A review and some hypotheses. In B. Schürch & J. Brozek (Eds.), *Malnutrition and behavior: A critical assessment of key issues*. Lausanne: Nestlé Foundation.

Engle, P. L., Yarbrough, C., & Klein, R. E. (1983). Sex differences in the effects of nutrition and social environment on mental development in rural Guatemala. In M. Buvinic, M. A. Lycette, & W. P. McGreevey (Eds.), *Women's issues in Third World poverty*. Baltimore: Johns Hopkins University Press.

Eysenck, H. J. (1986). The theory of intelligence and the psychophysiology of cognition. In R. J. Sternberg (Ed.), *Advances in the psychology of human intelligence* (Vol. 3). Hillsdale, NJ: Erlbaum.

Farran, D. C., & McKinney, J. D. (Eds.). (1986). *Risk in intellectual and psychosocial development*. Orlando, FL: Academic.

Freeman, E., Klein, R. E., Townsend, J. W., & Lechtig, A. (1980). Nutrition and cognitive development among rural Guatemalan children. *American Journal of Public Health, 70*, 1277–1285.

Garcia-Coll, C. (1990). Developmental outcome of minority infants: A process-oriented look into our beginnings. *Child Development, 61,* 270–289.

Geber, M., & Dean, R. F. A. (1955). Psychological factors in the etiology of kwashiorkor. *Bulletin of the World Health Organization, 12,* 471–475.

Geber, M., & Dean, R. F. A. (1956). The psychological changes accompanying kwashiorkor. *Courrier, 6,* 3–15.

Gibson, E. J. (1988). Exploratory behavior in the development of perceiving, acting, and the acquiring of knowledge. *Annual Review of Psychology, 39,* 1–41.

Gorman, K., & Pollitt, E. (1992). School efficiency in rural Guatemala. *International Review of Education, 38*(5), 519–534.

Gorman, K., & Pollitt, E. (1993). Determinants of school efficiency in Guatemala: Family background characteristics and early abilities. *International Journal of Behavioral Development, 16,* 75–91.

Grantham-McGregor, S., Meeks Gardner, J. M., Walker, S., & Powell, C. (1990). The relationship between undernutrition, activity levels and development in young children. In B. Schürch & N. S. Scrimshaw (Eds.), *Activity, energy expenditure and energy requirements of infants and children: Proceedings of an International Dietary Energy Consultative Group Workshop held in Cambridge, Massachusetts, USA November 14 to 17, 1989.* Lausanne: Nestlé Foundation.

Grantham-McGregor, S. M., Powell, C. A., Walker, S. P., & Himes, J. H. (1991). Nutritional supplementation, psychological stimulation and development of stunted children: The Jamaican study. *Lancet, 338*(8758), 1–5.

Graves, P. L. (1976). Nutrition, infant behavior, and maternal characteristics: A pilot study in West Bengal, India. *American Journal of Clinical Nutrition, 29,* 305–319.

Graves, P. L. (1978). Nutrition and infant behavior: A replication study in the Katmandu Valley, Nepal. *American Journal of Clinical Nutrition, 31,* 541–551.

Gustafson, G. E. (1984). Effects of the ability to locomote on infants' social and exploratory behaviors: An experimental study. *Developmental Psychology, 20,* 397–405.

Harper, L. V. (1970). Ontogenetic and phylogenetic functions of the parent-offspring relationship in mammals. *Advances in the Study of Behavior, 3,* 75–117.

Hebb, D. (1949). *Organization of behavior.* New York: Wiley.

Hertzig, M. E., Birch, H. G., Richardson, S. A., & Tizard, J. (1972). Intellectual levels of school children severely malnourished during the first two years of life. *Pediatrics, 49,* 814–823.

Hess, R. D., & Shipman, V. C. (1965). Early experience and the socialization of cognitive modes in children. *Child Development, 34,* 869–886.

Hess, R. D., & Shipman, V. C. (1967). Cognitive elements in maternal behavior. In J. P. Hill (Ed.), *Minnesota symposia on child psychology* (Vol. 2). Minneapolis: University of Minnesota Press.

Horowitz, F. D. (1987). *Exploring developmental theories: Towards a structural behavioral model of development.* Hillsdale, NJ: Erlbaum.

Hsueh, A. M., & Meyer, B. (1981). Maternal dietary supplementation and 5 year old Stanford Binet IQ test on the offspring in Taiwan. *Federation Proceedings, 40,* 897.

Hunt, J. McV. (1961). *Intelligence and experience.* New York: Ronald.

Husaini, M. A., Karyadi, L., Husaini, Y. K., Sandjaja, Karyadi, D., & Pollitt, E. (1991). Developmental effects of short-term supplementary feeding in nutritionally-at-risk Indonesian infants. *American Journal of Clinical Nutrition, 54,* 799–804.

Irwin, M., Engle, P. L., Yarbrough, C., Klein, R. E., & Townsend, J. (1978). The relationship of prior ability and family characteristics to school attendance and school achievement in rural Guatemala. *Child Development, 49,* 415–427.

Jelliffe, D. B. (1959). Protein-calorie malnutrition in tropical preschool children. *Journal of Pediatrics,* **54,** 227–256.

Jelliffe, D. B. (1965). Effect of malnutrition on behavioral and social development. In *Proceedings of the Western Hemisphere Nutrition Congress.* Chicago: American Medical Association.

Jensen, A. (1991, February). General mental ability: From psychometrics to biology. In T. J. Tighe (Chair), *Current conceptions of intelligence.* Symposium conducted at the meeting of the American Association for the Advancement of Science, Washington, DC.

Johnston, R. E., Low, S. M., de Baessa, Y., & MacVean, R. B. (1987). Interaction of nutritional and socioeconomic status as determinants of cognitive development in disadvantaged urban Guatemalan children. *American Journal of Physical Anthropology,* **73,** 501–506.

Joos, S. K., Pollitt, E., Mueller, W. H., & Albright, D. L. (1983). The Bacon Chow study: Maternal nutritional supplementation and infant behavioral development. *Child Development,* **54,** 669–676.

Klein, R. E., Arenales, P., Delgado, H., Engle, P., Guzman, G., Irwin, M., Lasky, R., Lechtig, A., Martorell, R., Mejía Pivaral, V., Russell, P., & Yarbrough, C. (1976). Effects of maternal nutrition on fetal growth and infant development. *Bulletin of the Pan American Health Organization,* **10,** 301–316.

Klein, R. E., Freeman, H. E., Spring, B., Nerlove, S. R., & Yarbrough, C. (1976). Cognitive test performance and indigenous conceptions of intelligence. *Journal of Psychology,* **93,** 273–279.

Konner, M. J. (1976). Maternal care, infant behavior, and development among the !Kung. In R. B. Lee & I. DeVore (Eds.), *Kalahari hunter-gatherers: Studies of the !Kung San and their neighbors.* Cambridge, MA: Harvard University Press.

Laosa, L. M. (1984). Social policies towards children of diverse ethnic, racial and language groups in the United States. In H. W. Stevenson & A. E. Siegel (Eds.), *Child development research and social policy.* Chicago: University of Chicago Press.

Lasky, R. E., Klein, R. E., Yarbrough, C., Engle, P. L., Lechtig, A., & Martorell, R. (1981). The relationship between physical growth and infant behavioral development in rural Guatemala. *Child Development,* **52,** 219–226.

Lasky, R. E., Klein, R. E., Yarbrough, C., & Kallio, K. D. (1981). The predictive validity of infant assessments in rural Guatemala. *Child Development,* **52,** 847–856.

Lechtig, A., Yarbrough, C., Delgado, H., Habicht, J.-P., Klein, R. E., & Martorell, R. (1975). Effects of moderate maternal malnutrition on birth weight. *American Journal of Clinical Nutrition,* **28,** 1223–1233.

Leiter, R. G. (1940). *The Leiter international performance scales* (Vol. 1). Santa Barbara, CA: Santa Barbara State College Press.

Levin, H. M., Pollitt, E., Galloway, R., & McGuire, J. (in press). Micronutrient deficiency disorders. In D. T. Jamison & W. H. Mosley (Eds.), *Evolving health sector priorities in developing countries.* New York: Oxford University Press, for the World Bank.

Levine, R. A., Levine, S. E., Richman, A., Tapia Uribe, F. M., Sunderland Correa, C., & Miller, P. M. (1991). Women's schooling and child care in demographic transition: A Mexican case study. *Population and Development Review,* **17**(3), 459–496.

Lozoff, B. (1988). Behavioral alterations in iron deficiency. *Advances in Pediatrics,* **35,** 331–360.

Lozoff, B., Klein, N. K., & Prabucki, K. M. (1986). Iron-deficient anemic infants at play. *Journal of Developmental and Behavioral Pediatrics,* **7**(3), 152–158.

Lutter, C. K., Mora, J. O., Habicht, J.-P., Rasmussen, K. M., Robson, D. S., Sellers, S. G., Super, C. M., & Herrera, M. G. (1989). Nutritional supplementation effects on child stunting because of diarrhea. *American Journal of Clinical Nutrition,* **50,** 1–8.

Maccoby, E., Dowley, E., Hagen, J., & Degerman, R. (1965). Activity level and intellectual functioning in normal preschool children. *Child Development, 36,* 761–770.

Manuel, H. T. (1967). *Technical reports, tests of general ability and tests of reading, Interamerican series.* San Antonio, TX: Guidance Testing Associates.

Martorell, R., & Habicht, J.-P. (1986). Growth in early childhood in developing countries. In F. Falkner & J. M. Tanner (Eds.), *Human growth: A comprehensive treatise* (2d ed., Vol. **3**). New York: Plenum.

Martorell, R., Habicht, J.-P., & Klein, R. W. (1982). Anthropometric indicators of changes in nutritional status in malnourished populations. In B. Underwood (Ed.), *Methodologies for human population studies in nutrition related to health, Bethesda, Maryland, July 24–25, 1979: Proceedings* (NIH Publication No. 82-2462). Washington, DC: U.S. Government Printing Office.

Martorell, R., Klein, R. E., & Delgado, H. (1980). Improved nutrition and its effects on anthropometric indicators of nutritional status. *Nutrition Reports International,* **21,** 219–230.

Martorell, R., Rivera, J., & Kaplowitz, H. (1990). Consequences of stunting in early childhood for adult body size in rural Guatemala. *Annales Nestlé,* **48,** 85–92.

Martorell, R., Rivera, J., Kaplowitz, H., & Pollitt, E. (1991, September). *Long-term consequences of growth retardation during early childhood.* Paper presented at the Sixth International Congress of Auxology, Madrid.

McLaren, D. S. (1974). The great protein fiasco. *Lancet,* **2**(7872), 93–96.

McLaren, D. S., Faris, R., & Zekian, B. (1968). The liver during recovery from protein-calorie malnutrition. *Journal of Tropical Medicine and Hygiene,* **71,** 271–281.

Meeks Gardner, J. M., Grantham-McGregor, S. M., Chang, S. M., & Powell, C. A. (1990). Dietary intake and observed activity of stunted and non-stunted children in Kingston, Jamaica: 2. Observed activity. *European Journal of Clinical Nutrition,* **44,** 585–593.

Moss, H. A. (1967). Sex, age, and state as determinants of mother-infant interaction. *Merrill-Palmer Quarterly,* **13,** 19–36.

National Research Council. (1989). *Recommended dietary allowances* (10th ed.). Washington, DC: National Academy Press.

Nerlove, S. B., Roberts, J. M., Klein, R. E., Yarbrough, C., & Habicht, J.-P. (1974). Natural indicators of cognitive development: An observational study of rural Guatemalan children. *Ethos,* **2,** 265–295.

Nicholls, E. E. (1923). Performance in certain mental tests of children classified as underweight and normal. *Journal of Comparative Psychology,* **3,** 147–179.

Piaget, J. (1952). *The origins of intelligence in children.* New York: International Universities Press. (Original work published in 1937)

Plomin, R., DeFries, J. C., & Loehlin, J. C. (1977). Genotypes-environment interaction and correlation in the analysis of human behavior. *Psychological Bulletin,* **84,** 309–322.

Pollitt, E. (1969). Ecology, malnutrition, and mental development. *Psychosomatic Medicine,* **31,** 193–200.

Pollitt, E. (1988). A critical view of three decades of research on the effects of chronic energy malnutrition on behavioral development. In B. Schürch & N. S. Scrimshaw (Eds.), *Chronic energy deficiency: Consequences and related issues: Proceedings of the meeting of the International Dietary Energy Consultative Group held in Guatemala City, Guatemala.* Lausanne: Nestlé Foundation.

Pollitt, E. (in press). Iron deficiency and cognitive function. *Annual Review of Nutrition.*

Pollitt, E., Garza, C., & Leibel, R. L. (1984). Nutrition and public policy. In H. W. Stevenson & A. E. Siegel (Eds.), *Child development research and social policy.* Chicago: University of Chicago Press.

Pollitt, E., & Granoff, D. (1967). Mental and motor development of Peruvian children tested for severe malnutrition. *Revista Interamericana de Psicologia*, **1**(2), 93–102.

Pollitt, E., & Oh, S.-Y. (1992). *Early supplementary feeding, infant development and health policy.* Unpublished manuscript.

Pollitt, E., & Ricciuti, H. (1969). Biological and social correlates of stature among children living in the slums of Lima, Peru. *American Journal of Orthopsychiatry*, **39**, 735–747.

Pollitt, E., & Thomson, C. (1977). Protein-calorie malnutrition and behavior: A view from psychology. In R. J. Wurtman & J. J. Wurtman (Eds.), *Nutrition and the brain* (Vol. **2**). New York: Raven.

Pryor, G. (1974). Malnutrition and the "critical period" hypothesis. In J. W. Prescott, M. S. Read, & D. B. Coursin (Eds.), *Brain function and malnutrition: Neuropsychological methods of assessment.* New York: Wiley.

Rath, R. (1959). Standardization of progressive matrices among college students. *Journal of Vocational and Educational Guidance*, **5**(4), 167–171.

Raven, J. C., Court, J. H., & Raven, J. (1984). *Manual for Raven's Progressive Matrices and Vocabulary Scales* (1983 ed.). London: H. K. Lewis.

Ricciuti, H. (1981). Developmental consequences of malnutrition in early childhood. In M. Lewis & N. Rosenblum (Eds.), *The uncommon child: The genesis of behavior* (Vol. **3**). New York: Plenum.

Rivera, J., & Castro, H. (1990, July). *Follow-up study: Design and description; Data collection: Organization, coverage, sample size.* Paper presented at the Rockefeller Foundation Conference on the Guatemala Follow-Up Study, Bellagio.

Rosenzweig, M. R. (1966). Environmental complexity, cerebral change, and behavior. *American Psychologist*, **21**, 321–332.

Ruel, M. (1991). *Methodology to derive socioeconomic factors for 1975 and 1988.* Unpublished manuscript.

Rush, D., Horvitz, D. G., Seaver, W. B., Alvir, J. M., Garbowski, G. C., Leighton, J., Sloan, N. L., Johnson, S. S., Kulka, R. A., & Shanklin, D. S. (1988). Background and introduction: The national WIC evaluation: Evaluation of the special supplemental food program for women, infants and children. *American Journal of Clinical Nutrition*, **48**(Suppl.), 389–393.

Rush, D., Stein, Z., & Susser, M. (Eds.). (1980). *Diet in pregnancy: A randomized controlled trial of nutritional supplements.* New York: Alan R. Liss.

Rutishauser, H. E., & Whitehead, R. G. (1972). Energy intake and expenditure in 1–3 year old Ugandan children living in a rural environment. *British Journal of Nutrition*, **28**, 145–152.

Rutter, M., & Pickles, A. (1991). Person-environment interactions: Concepts, mechanisms, and implications for data analysis. In T. D. Wachs & R. Plomin (Eds.), *Conceptualization and measurement of organism-environment interaction.* Washington, DC: American Psychological Association.

Salkind, N. J., & Wright, J. C. (1977). The development of reflection-impulsivity and cognitive efficiency. *Human Development*, **20**, 377–387.

Sameroff, A. J., & Chandler, M. J. (1975). Reproductive risk and the continuum of caretaking casualty. In F. D. Horowitz (Ed.), *Reviews of child development research* (Vol. **4**). Chicago: University of Chicago Press.

SAS. (1988). *SAS/STAT User's Guide* (6.03 ed.). Cary, NC: SAS Institute.

Schroeder, D. G., Kaplowitz, H., & Martorell, R. (1992). *Patterns and predictions of attendance and consumption of supplement in an intervention study in rural Guatemala.* Unpublished manuscript.

Scott, J. P. (1962). Critical periods in behavioral development. *Science*, **138**, 949–958.

Scrimshaw, N. S. (1969). Early malnutrition and central nervous system function. *Merrill-Palmer Quarterly,* **15,** 375–383.

Scrimshaw, N. S., & Gordon, J. E. (Eds.). (1968). *Malnutrition, learning and behavior.* Cambridge, MA: MIT Press.

Sigman, M., Neumann, C., Carter, E., Cattle, D. J., D'Souza, S., & Bwibo, N. (1988). Home interactions and the development of Embu toddlers in Kenya. *Child Development,* **59,** 1251–1261.

Sigman, M., Neumann, C., Jansen, A. A. J., & Bwibo, N. (1989). Cognitive abilities of Kenyan children in relation to nutrition, family characteristics and education. *Child Development,* **60**(6), 1463–1474.

Simonson, M., Sherwin, R. W., Anilane, J. K., Yu, W. K., & Chow, B. F. (1969). Neuromotor development in progeny of underfed mother rats. *Journal of Nutrition,* **98,** 18–22.

Sternberg, S. (1966). High-speed scanning in human memory. *Science,* **153,** 652–654.

Stoch, M. B., & Smythe, P. M. (1963). Does undernutrition during infancy inhibit brain growth and subsequent intellectual development? *Archives of Disease in Childhood,* **38,** 546–552.

Suchman, E. A. (1968). Sociocultural factors in nutritional studies. In D. C. Glass (Ed.), *Environmental influences.* New York: Rockefeller University Press/Russell Sage.

Super, C. M., Herrera, M. G., & Mora, J. O. (1990). Long-term effects of food supplementation and psychosocial intervention on the physical growth of Colombian infants at risk of malnutrition. *Child Development,* **61,** 29–49.

Super, C. M., Herrera, M. G., & Mora, J. O. (1991, April). *Cognitive outcomes of early nutritional intervention in the Bogotá study.* Paper presented at the meeting of the Society for Research in Child Development, Seattle.

Townsend, J. W., Klein, R. E., Irwin, M. H., Owens, W., Yarbrough, C., & Engle, P. L. (1982). Nutrition and preschool mental development. In D. A. Wagner & H. W. Stevenson (Eds.), *Cross-cultural perspectives on child development.* San Francisco: Freeman.

Trivers, R. L. (1974). Parent-offspring conflict. *American Zoologist,* **14,** 249–264.

Vasquez-Velasquez, L. (1988). Energy expenditure and physical activity of malnourished Gambian infants. *Proceedings of the Nutritional Society,* **47,** 233–239.

Vernon, P. A. (Ed.). (1987). *Speed of information-processing and intelligence.* Norwood, NJ: Ablex.

Waber, D. P., Vuori-Christiansen, L., Ortiz, N., Clement, J. R., Christiansen, N. E., Mora, J. O., Reed, R. B., & Herrera, M. G. (1981). Nutritional supplementation, maternal education, and cognitive development of infants at risk of malnutrition. *American Journal of Clinical Nutrition,* **34,** 807–813.

Wachs, T. (1990). Temperament, activity and behavioral development of infants and children. In B. Schürch & N. S. Scrimshaw (Eds.), *Activity, energy expenditure and energy requirements of infants and children: Proceedings of an International Dietary Energy Consultative Group Workshop held in Cambridge, Massachusetts, USA November 14 to 17, 1989.* Lausanne: Nestlé Foundation.

Wachs, T. D. (1992). *The nature of nurture: Individual differences and development series* (Vol. 3). Newbury Park, CA: Sage.

Wachs, T. D., & Plomin, R. S. (Eds.). (1991). *Conceptualization and measurement of organism-environment interaction.* Washington, DC: American Psychological Association.

Werner, E. E. (1986). The concept of risk from a developmental perspective. In B. K. Keogh (Ed.), *Advances in special education: Vol. 4. Developmental problems in infancy and the preschool years.* Greenwich, CT: JAI.

Werner, E. E., Bierman, J. M., & French, F. E. (1971). *The children of Kauai.* Honolulu: University of Hawaii Press.

Werner, E. E., & Smith, R. S. (1977). *Kauai's children come of age.* Honolulu: University of Hawaii Press.

Werner, E. E., & Smith, R. S. (1982). *Vulnerable but invincible: A longitudinal study of resilient children and youth.* New York: McGraw-Hill.

Werner, E. E., & Smith, R. S. (1992). *Overcoming the odds: High risk children from birth to adulthood.* Ithaca, NY: Cornell University Press.

Williams, C. D. (1933). A nutritional disease of childhood associated with a maize diet. *Archives of Disease in Childhood,* **8,** 423–433.

Witkin, H. A., Dyk, R. B., Faterson, H. F., Goodenough, D. R., & Karp, S. A. (1962). *Psychological differentiation.* New York: Wiley.

ACKNOWLEDGMENTS

Data collection and analyses were supported by National Institutes of Health (NIH) grant HD22440 and by Pew Charitable Trusts grant 90-00210-000. The NIH study was a collaborative effort involving investigators from several institutions: R. Martorell (principal investigator, then at Stanford University, now at Cornell University), J. Rivera (Institute of Nutrition of Central America and Panama, Guatemala City), E. Pollitt (University of California, Davis), and J. Haas (Cornell University).

We gratefully acknowledge the valuable comments on earlier versions of this manuscript from Curt Acredolo, Janet Peerson, Henry Ricciuti, and the anonymous reviewers. Their time and thoughtful input are greatly appreciated. We also wish to acknowledge the contributions made by Dr. Robert Klein. As director of the longitudinal phase (1969–1977), he built the basis for the follow-up study that began in 1988. An earlier comprehensive discussion among experts in the International Dietary Energy Consultative Group contributed substantially to the data presented in this *Monograph*.

GOING BEYOND NUTRITION:
NUTRITION, CONTEXT, AND DEVELOPMENT

Theodore D. Wachs

Demographic data have indicated that undernutrition is a common occurrence for a large proportion of the world's children (Simeon & Grantham-McGregor, 1990). Evidence relating undernutrition to cognitive development has been available for at least half a century (Brozek, 1978). In spite of these facts, interest by behavioral researchers in the role of nutritional influences on development has been relatively limited, at least as indicated by available publications on this topic. For example, a Psychlit scan between 1987 and 1992 revealed only 14 references on the topic of nutrition and cognitive ability, with only seven of these references involving children. In contrast, a Psychlit scan of studies relating genetics to cognitive ability yielded 67 studies, 42 of which involved children. It is not clear why behavioral researchers have tended to neglect the study of nutrition. Perhaps the fact that the bulk of studies on behavioral development have been done by researchers from developed countries (Schopflin & Muller-Brettel, 1990) may have something to do with this relative neglect of links between nutrition and behavioral development. It is to be hoped that the present *Monograph* will go a long way toward remedying this state of benign neglect.

Contributions of the Monograph

There are two major findings that emerge from this data set. First, there is evidence that early nutritional supplementation can have long-term developmental consequences for later cognitive performance. If developmental researchers wish to understand processes influencing variability in cognitive development in populations other than *advantaged children in West-*

ern developed countries, the present pattern of results strongly argues for the development of models that include nutritional status as a critical parameter.[1]

The second major finding of this study is that the relation of nutrition to concurrent and later cognitive performance does not fit a simple main-effects model. Rather, the relation of nutrition to cognitive performance is moderated both by the time period during which the nutritional supplementation was given and by the larger sociodemographic context (social status, school level) within which subjects resided. For example, children in the lowest sociodemographic groups benefited more from nutritional supplementation than did children from higher sociodemographic groups. Similarly, while there were still nutritional influences when supplementation was started after 2 years of age, the effect appears to be less powerful. What these results illustrate is the need to look at nutritional influences as part of a *system* of multiple determinants (Wachs, 1993).

The results outlined above also emphasize the need to tailor our data analysis strategies to recognize the operation of this multidetermined system. For example, ecological theorists such as Bronfenbrenner (1993) have contended that traditional analytic approaches for dealing with individual characteristics or contextual factors, namely, by covarying or partialing them out, are inappropriate. Covariance or partialing techniques are based on the assumption that the same developmental processes occur for different individuals or within different contexts (Bronfenbrenner, 1993). The present findings are a dramatic demonstration as to why it is important to look for different developmental processes across different contexts, rather than assuming that the same main-effect process is operating across contexts. Had Pollitt et al. not tested for moderating sociodemographic or grade-level influences, they might well have come to the conclusion that increased nutrition enhances development for their total sample; this conclusion, although parsimonious, would have been highly misleading. Given increasing evidence that most behavioral variability within normal ranges appears to be multidetermined, both at the molecular level (Plomin, 1990) and at a molar level (Wachs, 1993), the present results offer further confirmation as to why it is important to consider and not control for multiple influences on development.

The present project offers not only a set of findings that emphasize the need to bridge the gap between nutritional and developmental research but

---

[1] While we tend to think of undernutrition as a phenomenon found primarily in less developed countries, it is important to remember that pockets of undernourished populations are also found in Western developed countries (Karp, in press). Hence, the present findings may also be relevant for understanding group differences in cognition in developed countries as well.

also a model of how a nutritional intervention field study should be carried out. This study is exemplary in terms of the care taken to identify potential confounders and, where possible, test for the effect of these potential confounders. Where it is impossible to test, Pollitt et al. are explicit in terms of how potential confounders might affect their results. There are multiple examples that illustrate why this study may be considered as a model nutritional intervention study. These include testing whether the supplement was truly a supplement and not just a substitution, looking for selective migration effects, considering whether attendance at the feeding station could act as a placebo, and testing for examiner effects. What we have here is not only a most provocative data set but also a set of guidelines for how future studies of this type should be designed and implemented.

Unresolved Issues

Methodological Issues

One interesting finding is that nutritional interventions had a much more dramatic effect on psychometric measures of intelligence and achievement than on information-processing measures, such as reaction time. A similar pattern of differential influence is shown for the effects of SES and schooling. These differences could have important theoretical considerations. It has been argued that information-processing measures may be more universal (hard wired) and therefore potentially less responsive to extraneous factors such as nutrition, schooling, or sociodemographic differences (Kail, 1991). However, before assuming that this differential reactivity of psychometric versus information-processing measures reflects differential wiring, we must consider at least one alternative explanation. As Pollitt et al. show in their Table 13, the psychometric and achievement measures were more stable than the information-processing measures. The lower degree of intervention effects for the information-processing measures may not reflect differential reactivity as much as the fact that information-processing measures may be less stable.[2] While this study was not designed to test cognitive theory issues of this type, it is unfortunate that less stable information-processing measures did result in a loss of potentially interesting information. This may suggest the need to build in compensatory procedures such as *aggregation* (Rushton, Brainerd, & Pressley, 1983) to com-

---

[2] As a preliminary test of this hypothesis, I correlated stability coefficients for information-processing measures (Table 13) with the beta coefficients reflecting nutritional treatment effects on these five measures (Table 19). The resulting correlation, although modest ($r = .26$), is in the expected direction, suggesting stronger effect sizes for the more stable measures.

pensate for potential stability differences when researchers suspect the possibility of differential stability for measures from different domains.

A second question involves sex differences. While Pollitt et al. take great care to look for sex differences in the preschool period and in terms of village demographics, there is a surprising omission in the follow-up data. Specifically, there is no evidence presented on whether there are sex differences in either school attendance or school progress. This omission is particularly surprising given the fact that there are sex differences favoring males in the results (see Tables 18 and 19) as well as results indicating the relevance of school factors to subsequent cognitive performance. It could be argued that, since the sex × treatment interaction was nonsignificant, looking at sex differences in school functioning is, at best, only a side issue. However, as elegantly demonstrated by Wahlsten (1990), analyzing for interactions often results in lower statistical power than analyzing for main effects. Under these circumstances, if males have higher levels of school attendance and school progress, it would be useful to consider the potential role of sex differences in understanding processes underlying nutrition-cognition relations. This is particularly true if there were also sex differences in *consumption of the supplement* as opposed just to attendance at the feeding station.

Conceptual Issues

In their discussion, Pollitt et al. emphasize the protective (buffering) effects of supplementation. In fact, what the present results strongly suggest is *double buffering,* in the sense that both supplementation and favorable sociodemographic context can each act as a buffer. Specifically, if we look within supplementation groups, the lack of SES differences in the Atole condition clearly shows nutritional buffering, as do the differences between the Atole and the Fresco groups at the lowest SES level. However, if we look between conditions, the lack of Atole and Fresco differences at the upper-SES levels clearly shows that sociodemographic contextual factors can also act as a buffer for those children who are not nutritionally supplemented.[3]

---

[3] Relations between social class, nutrition, and cognition suggest the operation of a buffering process, wherein enhanced nutrition can protect against the risk of low socioeconomic status while the protective factors that covary with high socioeconomic status can buffer against the detrimental influence of inadequate nutrition. In contrast, when we look at the relation between school achievement level, nutrition, and developmental outcome, buffering does not appear to be operating; children in the Fresco condition who achieve high grade levels do not necessarily show superior cognitive performance over Fresco children who do not achieve high grade levels. Rather, what appears to be operating here

The potential influence of context becomes even more critical when we look at the explanation offered as to why early nutritional supplementation influences were maintained and expanded across time. Basically, Pollitt et al. favor a two-process model, as shown in Figure C1a. First, they propose that early nutritional differences lead to differences in physical growth; physical growth differences, in turn, influence how children are subsequently treated (e.g., smaller children are treated as younger than their chronological age, whereas larger, more mature-looking children are allowed more autonomy and independence). It is this differential treatment that is proposed as one mechanism wherein the effect of early nutritional supplementation is maintained across time. Support for certain aspects of this model comes from data other than those described in the present *Monograph*. For example, in both Egypt and Kenya, variability in caregiver behaviors toward 18–30-month-old toddlers was associated primarily with the level of *toddler nutritional intake* rather than with the level of caregiver intake, thus demonstrating that differences in children's nutrition do relate to how children are treated (Wachs et al., 1992). Supporting the hypothesis that less adequately nourished children are treated as if they were younger, in Kenya, and to a lesser extent in Egypt, inadequately nourished toddlers were carried and held more by caregivers; toddlers who were carried and held more showed lower levels of cognitive and behavioral competence.

The second aspect of the proposed model involves higher nutritional status resulting in increased physical activity. Increased physical activity in turn results in increased exploratory behavior, which, in turn, enhances subsequent cognitive development (see Fig. C1a). Again, support for this model is found in other sources. Previous research has clearly established linkages between nutrition and activity, between activity and exploration (Schürch & Scrimshaw, 1991), and between exploration and cognitive development (Wachs, 1992).

Where the proposed model may be problematic is not so much in its general outline but rather in terms of not also considering the possibility that *higher-order contextual effects* (e.g., culture) may influence how nutritionally at-risk children are treated. Specifically, in the two-country study referred to above, the data from Kenya indicate that poorly fed children not only are carried more but are also responded *more* to by caregivers; in contrast, in Egypt, caregivers were *less responsive* to poorly fed children (Wachs et al., 1992). These cross-cultural differences between Kenya and Egypt may reflect differences in level of food intake in the two countries—

---

is a *synergistic process*, wherein maximum performance is achieved with a combination of nutritional supplementation plus success in school. This illustrates how different predictor-criterion combinations may be governed by different underlying processes.

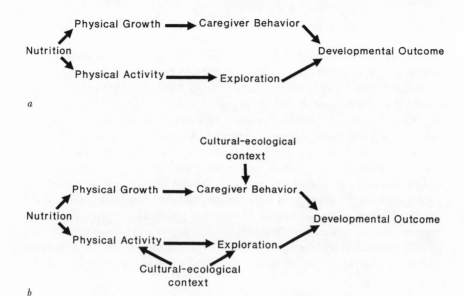

Fig. C1.—*a*, Nutrition model. *b*, Nutrition-context model

Kenyan toddlers had significantly lower food intake than Egyptian toddlers. The fact that the nutritional level in Guatemala appears to be closer to that of Kenya than of Egypt suggests that this aspect of the authors' model may be valid for nutritional-contextual situations in which there is moderate malnutrition and where cultures support caregivers' attempts to compensate for inadequate intake by special treatment of the physically smaller child. However, the model may be less applicable in a context like Egypt, where food is more available and where poorly fed toddlers may come from families that are less able to provide for the toddlers' needs in multiple areas of development, including both nutrition and adequacy of caregiving. The critical point is that how undernourished children are treated appears to be a function not only of physical growth but also of cultural differences, suggesting a model more like that shown in Figure C1*b*.

A similar point can be made in regard to the nutrition-activity-exploration link. In a number of societies, infants' physical activity and attempts to explore the environment are likely to be *restricted* by their caregivers, either as a function of heavy maternal work loads or as a function of naturally occurring environmental hazards (Brazelton, Robey, & Collier, 1969; Kaplan & Dove, 1987; McSwain, 1981; Super, 1981). In contrast to the model postulated by the authors, in which higher levels of nutrition result in higher levels of motor behavior, which result in higher levels of exploration, in some cultures more adequately nourished children might find their attempts at motor exploration sharply restricted by their caregivers (see Fig. C1b). As a result, we would not necessarily expect a developmental advantage in some cultures for more adequately nourished, physically active children. As the authors themselves note, the child's capacity to modulate higher activity on the basis of contextual demands may be more critical than high levels of activity per se.

The alternative model offered in Figure C1b should not be seen as contradicting the main point of the model offered by Pollitt et al. I believe that they are essentially correct in suggesting that one path linking early undernutrition to later deficits in cognitive performance is mediated via child behaviors and caregiver reactivity. What I am suggesting is that the model needs to be taken one step further, namely, integrating contextual factors. Higher-order contextual factors can influence whether caregivers respond in developmentally facilitative or inhibitory ways toward more adequately nourished children; these factors can also influence the degree to which caregivers support or inhibit the child's attempts at activity and exploratory behaviors.

Implications

The results of the present project are rich, not only in terms of the actual results, but also in terms of the implications of these results for future research, theory, and intervention with children at risk.

Research Implications

In their initial review of the study of nutrition-behavior relations, Pollitt et al. note the possibility that critical nutritional parameters may involve *micronutrients* (e.g., vitamins, trace minerals) rather than energy (kilocalories) or macronutrients (e.g., protein). They also discuss some of the reasons why more recent nutrition-behavior research has shifted to experimental field studies rather than correlational studies. However, if the critical nutrient parameters are micronutrients, this raises the question of *which micronutrients or combinations of micronutrients* are likely to be most salient in influencing developmental variability. Correlational studies may be initially useful in dealing with this question, through assessing which micronutrients or micronutrient combinations are most consistently related to developmental variability. To the extent that correlational studies can also measure and test the role of nonnutritional covariates (e.g., morbidity, sociodemographic risk factors, caregiver behaviors), these types of studies also may be extremely useful in illustrating the nature of the multidetermined system of influences encountered by the child who is at nutritional risk. Correlational studies could form the basis for future intervention-supplementation studies, designed to separate out correlational from causal relations between nutrition, nutritional covariates, and development.

A second implication involves the finding that the effect of nutritional supplementation will be moderated by contextual factors, such as sociodemographic status and school attendance. I have noted previously in this Commentary the importance of looking at supplementation effects at different contextual levels rather than assuming that *one supplement feeds all.* Such a strategy illustrates the process by context design, as described by Bronfenbrenner (1993). However, I would go further and argue that this pattern of results can also illustrate the importance of looking at individual differences in reaction to treatment (nutrition or otherwise), within a given contextual level. In spite of the fact that there are marked individual differences in response to similar treatment regimens, including both biological and psychological interventions, the study of these types of individual differences in reactivity to treatment has been a relatively neglected area in the behavioral sciences (Wachs & Plomin, 1991). It will be important to continue looking at the degree to which contexts moderate treatment effects. However, it will be of equal importance not only to look at mean differences in reaction to treatment but also to look for variability in response to treatment *within a given context level.* For example, for low-SES children who are nutritionally supplemented in the first 2 years, what are the characteristics that distinguish those children who benefit more from supplementation from those who benefit less? This next step leads into what Bronfenbrenner (1993) has called a *person by process by context* research strategy.

One obvious drawback of person by process by context research is sample size, in the sense that, the more subsamples, the fewer subjects at each subsample, and the lower the power. To some extent, we may be able to compensate for potentially lower power by increased use of aggregation, more precise measurement of critical variables, and utilization of statistical procedures targeted at specific subgroup/individual effects (for a discussion of these issues, see Wachs & Plomin, 1991). Further, as shown in both the present *Monograph* and previously published work by Werner on resilient children (Werner & Smith, 1982), what we lose in power may be more than made up for by the richness of data obtained.

Theoretical Implications

As noted earlier, the present results clearly emphasize the importance of going beyond main-effect approaches when developing models for understanding the nature of nutrition-development relations. Multidimensional multidetermined systems approaches seem to offer a much better fit to the data. Examples of these types of approaches have been developed not only for the study of nutrition per se (Pollitt, 1988) but also for the more general area of "determinants" of development (Bronfenbrenner, 1993; Horowitz, 1987; Wachs, 1992).

The present results also have implications for the question of sensitive periods in human development. Available reviews suggest that there is no strong evidence for a critical period in human development and only limited evidence for sensitive periods (Bornstein, 1989). While the sample size for the late exposure group was relatively small, the present results at least suggest the possibility of the continued, although diminishing, salience of nutritional interventions when started after 2 years of age. These results do not support a critical periods notion, but they are not inconsistent with theories based on periods of maximum sensitivity, in the sense that, while earlier may be better, later may still offer some benefits.

Implications for Intervention

Particularly in less developed countries, theoretically based research is seen as having less value than research that has practical implications for individuals' day-to-day lives (Nsamenang, 1992). Pollitt et al. clearly share this concern, as exemplified by their discussion of public policy issues. A major policy issue that comes from the present research is the question of which children should be targeted for nutritional intervention. In an era of increasingly scarce resources, can we afford to target all children who are potentially at risk, or should interventions target primarily those children who are most at risk? If the latter, which children? In the present project, maximum risk appears to occur for those children who are simultaneously exposed to inadequate nutrition (no supplementation), low social class, and low levels of school attainment (the three-way interaction demonstrated with Raven's Progressive Matrices).

Clearly, the present results suggest the importance of targeting low-socioeconomic-status children for nutritional intervention. Providing nutritional supplementation for these children can be seen as one way of breaking the naturally occurring covariance between inadequate rearing environments and inadequate nutrition. However, Pollitt et al. go beyond low SES and also argue for the importance of considering grade attainment as another potential risk factor that may call for nutritional intervention. Their argument is based, in part, on the synergistic interaction between treatment and grade level as well as on the assumption that, even at the upper levels of the SES distribution, there may be only a limited amount of buffering that a poor rural environment can offer to a child. In contrast, I would argue that the data presented in this *Monograph* seem to suggest that *supplementation* should be directed primarily toward low-SES children.

There are two reasons for emphasizing SES. First, in contrast to the authors' argument that there is only so much environmental buffering that can be offered to children in a poor rural community, the SES buffering effects for Fresco children show that something positive is being offered to children, even within this relatively restricted context. Second, the results at least suggest a diminishing effect of nutritional intervention when started after 2 years of age. If the strongest effects of nutrition are shown for children in the first 2 years of life, then the only possible targeting is social class since at-risk children are not yet enrolled in school. What the present results could suggest is a two-stage process. In the first stage, nutritional intervention would be directed primarily toward children in the lowest social class groups. In the second stage, after children reach school age, there should be a secondary emphasis on *economic aid to families*, to allow supplemented children to remain in school as long as possible.

Conclusions

The present project is a major contribution to the literature, not only in terms of demonstrating that early nutritional supplementation can have long-term effects on cognition, but also in terms of illustrating potential processes whereby nutritional influences interact with the overall context within which the individual functions. There has been a slowly increasing emphasis in the literature on biological and contextual linkages. Most of our current efforts in this direction have involved linkages between genes and environments (e.g., Plomin & McClearn, in press). The present results suggest that an equally fruitful path may lie in exploring linkages between nutrition, context, and the implication of these linkages for developmental variability.

References

Bornstein, M. (1989). Sensitive periods in development. *Psychological Bulletin, 105,* 179–197.

Brazelton, T., Robey, J., & Collier, G. (1969). Infant development in the Zinacanteco Indians of southern Mexico. *Pediatrics, 4,* 274–309.

Bronfenbrenner, U. (1993). Ecological system theory. In R. Wozniak & K. Fisher (Eds.), *Specific environments: Thinking in contexts.* Hillsdale, NJ: Erlbaum.

Brozek, J. (1978). Nutrition, malnutrition and behavior. *Annual Reviews of Psychology, 29,* 157–178.

Horowitz, F. (1987). *Exploring developmental theories.* Hillsdale, NJ: Erlbaum.

Kail, R. (1991). Development of processing speed in childhood and adolescence. *Advances in Child Development and Behavior, 23,* 151–185.

Kaplan, H., & Dove, H. (1987). Infant development among the Ache in Eastern Paraguay. *Developmental Psychology, 23,* 109–198.

Karp, R. (in press). *Malnourished children in the United States: Caught in the cycle of poverty.* New York: Springer.

McSwain, R. (1981). Care and conflict in infant development. *Infant Behavior and Development,* **4,** 225–246.

Nsamenang, A. (1992). *Human development in cultural contexts.* Newbury Park, CA: Sage.

Plomin, R. (1990). The role of inheritance in behavior. *Science,* **248,** 183–188.

Plomin, R., & McClearn, G. (in press). *Nature, nurture and psychology.* Washington, DC: American Psychological Association.

Pollitt, E. (1988). A critical view of three decades of research on the effects of chronic malnutrition on behavioral development. In B. Schürch & N. Scrimshaw (Eds.), *Chronic energy deficiency: Consequences and related issues.* Lausanne: International Dietary Energy Consultative Group.

Rushton, P., Brainerd, C., & Pressley, M. (1983). Behavioral development and construct validity: The principle of aggregation. *Psychological Bulletin,* **94,** 18–38.

Schopflin, U., & Muller-Brettel, M. (1990). *International Journal of Behavioral Development:* Scope and trends. *International Journal of Behavioral Development,* **13,** 393–406.

Schürch, B., & Scrimshaw, N. (Eds.). (1991). *Activity, energy expenditure and energy requirement of infants and children.* Lausanne: International Dietary Energy Consultative Group.

Simeon, D., & Grantham-McGregor, S. (1990). Nutritional deficiencies and children's behavioral and mental development. *Nutrition Research Review,* **3,** 1–24.

Super, C. (1981). Behavioral development in infancy. In R. H. Munroe, R. L. Munroe, & B. Whiting (Eds)., *Handbook of cross-cultural human development.* New York: Garland.

Wachs, T. D. (1992). *The nature of nurture.* Newbury Park, CA: Sage.

Wachs, T. D. (1993). Determinants of intellectual development: Single determinant research in a multi-determinant universe. *Intelligence,* **17,** 1–9.

Wachs, T. D., & Plomin, R. (1991). *Conceptualization and measurement of organism-environment interaction.* Washington, DC: American Psychological Association.

Wachs, T. D., Sigman, M., Bishry, Z., Moussa, W., Jerome, N., Neumann, C., Bwibo, N., & McDonald, M. (1992). Caregiver child interaction patterns in two cultures in relation to nutrition. *International Journal of Behavioral Development,* **15,** 1–18.

Wahlsten, D. (1990). Insensitivity of the analysis of variance to heredity-environment interactions. *Behavior and Brain Sciences,* **13,** 109–161.

Werner, E., & Smith, R. (1982). *Vulnerable but invincible.* New York: McGraw-Hill.

EARLY SUPPLEMENTARY FEEDING AND COGNITION:
A RETROSPECTIVE COMMENT

Nevin S. Scrimshaw

Three common nutritional deficiencies are now recognized to have the potential for permanent adverse effects on learning and behavior, those of protein-energy deficiency, iron, and iodine. The lasting effects of protein-energy malnutrition began to be recognized from studies in the 1950s and those of iron in the late 1960s. Although feeble-minded dwarfs have been associated with maternal iodine deficiency for more than 50 years, convincing evidence of lesser degrees of neurological damage due to iodine deficiency during the first and second trimester of pregnancy was first presented only in the 1970s. For both iron and chronic protein-energy deficiencies, permanent damage can occur in infancy and early childhood.

The severe acute deficiency of protein relative to calories that results in kwashiorkor is characterized by a profound apathy that responds relatively rapidly to a therapeutic diet. However, cognitive tests of children who had recovered from kwashiorkor gave evidence of continuing impairment. These long-term effects seemed to be due, not to the acute episode of kwashiorkor, but to the duration and severity of the marasmus on which the acute episode of kwashiorkor is usually superimposed (Yatkin & McClaren, 1970). Most cases of kwashiorkor occur after the first year of life as a consequence of poor weaning practices and concurrent infections.

When marasmus develops in infants and young children as the result of a chronic lack of both dietary energy and protein, it produces lasting effects on cognition, although these can be moderated by refeeding and psychosocial stimulation (Grantham-McGregor, Stewart, & Schofield, 1980). Decreased cognitive function with partial starvation in adults was a consistent finding in the World War II studies of Keys, Brozek, Henschel, Mickelsen, and Taylor (1959). Among the many countries from which lasting cognitive effects have been described as the result of kwashiorkor and marasmus are Chile (Monckeberg, 1968), India (Champakam, Srikantia, & Gopalan, 1968), Jamaica (Grantham-McGregor, Powell, Walker, & Himes, 1991), Lebanon (Hoorweg & Piaget, 1977), Mexico (Gomez, Velasco, Ramos, Cravioto, & Frenk, 1954), Peru (Pollitt & Granoff, 1967), Uganda (Gerber & Dean, 1967), and Yugoslavia (Yatkin & McClaren, 1970).

Cravioto and his colleagues (Cravioto & DeLicardie, 1968; Cravioto, DeLicardie, & Birch, 1966) deserve credit for demonstrating that subclinical malnutrition manifested only by impaired growth can affect behavior. Among lower socioeconomic groups in both Mexico and Guatemala, preschool children in the lowest quartile of weight for age had significantly poorer performances on various tests of intersensory perception than did those in the highest quartile. For children of university faculty and other professionals in middle- and upper-income groups in the two countries, there was no relation with weight quartile. The extent to which the differences were due to the lesser sensory stimulation of children of the poorest families rather than the biological consequences of a poor diet and infections could not be determined at the time.

In March 1967, the international conference "Malnutrition, Learning and Behavior," held in Cambridge, Massachusetts, brought together for the first time four overlapping disciplinary groups—nutritionists and behavioral scientists, some working with experimental animals and others with human subjects (Scrimshaw & Gordon, 1968). The evidence presented at the meeting that malnutrition in the infant animal could impair performance on behavioral tests was incontrovertible. So was the experimental evidence for a permanent effect of early malnutrition on the brain structure and functioning of these animals. It was also clear that lack of the stimulation could have similar effects and that stimulation could, at least partially, prevent the effects of malnutrition.

The coexistence of social deprivation and malnutrition, characteristic of children in low income groups, was not confounding in the work with experimental animals. However, in studies of children, the influence of the two factors could not be separated, and the conference was unable to resolve this dilemma. Moreover, the anatomical evidence of neurological change in malnourished children was weak except for a correlation with head circumference.

An early study frequently cited at the time, that of Stoch and Smythe (1968) in South Africa, was invalid because the malnourished and control groups were from quite different social and economic strata. Even in those studies in which the malnourished and control groups were carefully matched for socioeconomic status, the stimulating effects of the supplement were not taken into account.

The 1967 conference stimulated a number of now classic studies in developing-country populations. In Bogota (Mora, Herrera, Sellers, & Ortiz, 1981), children from poor families received either food supplementation for the entire family, from mid-pregnancy until the target child was 3 years old, or a twice-weekly home visiting program, from birth to 3 years, to promote cognitive development. At 3 years of age, children who received the food supplementation averaged 2.6 cm and 642 grams larger than controls. Supplementation resulted in small but significant improvement in Bayley test scores. Similar findings were reported from a study by Bacon Chow in Taiwan (Adair & Pollitt, 1985).

In Cali, preschool slum children received 1–4 years of combined supplementation and stimulation daily (Sinisterra, McKay, McKay, Gomez, & Korgi, 1977). Although each additional year brought a significant improvement in cognitive test performance, final scores were 20% lower than in children of middle- and upper-income families not enrolled in the program, even after 4 years (McKay, Sinisterra, McKay, Gomez, & Lloreda, 1978). The experimental design did not permit identifying the role of malnutrition alone.

Two important studies were begun at that time, one in Guatemala at the Institute of Nutrition of Central America and Panama (INCAP) (Klein, Irwin, Engel, & Yarbrough, 1977), described in this *Monograph,* and the other in Mexico by the National Institute of Nutrition (Chavez & Martinez, 1982). Both were well designed, and both strongly confirmed that poor rural breast-fed children who received a protein-calorie supplement up to 2 years of age were taller, had fewer infections, and performed better on appropriate cognitive tests than children receiving only social stimulation.

In Guatemala, the experimental and control groups were in different villages, introducing a possible confounding factor. However, in Mexico, after the base-line studies, half the children in the village of Tezonteopan, selected randomly, received a supplement of flavored milk and added vitamins and minerals. All the children in this study received stimulation visits and medical care. In Guatemala, the comparison was between groups receiving a beverage rich in protein and energy (Atole) and groups receiving a protein-free, low-calorie drink (Fresco). In both the Guatemalan and the Mexican studies, growth and performance on behavioral tests were significantly greater in the supplemented group. It is unlikely, therefore, that the results of the initial study in Guatemala described in this *Monograph* are an artifact due to chance differences among the study villages.

Both studies were planned to minimize the confounding effects of social stimulus during delivery of the nutritional supplement. However, the design of these two seminal studies made it impossible to know what the situation would have been with no intervention at all. It is highly probable that the benefits of nutritional supplementation (compared with doing nothing at all) were underestimated because any supplementation also provides increased stimulation. It should also be noted that the differences between the Atole and the Fresco control groups in this study were due to the higher protein content of the Atole. The Fresco was very low in calories as well as protein free, but, since about three times as much of it was consumed per person, caloric intakes were similar.

Demonstrating the improvement in cognitive performance of infants and young children whose mothers had been supplemented and who have been given additional nutritious food during and after weaning is in itself an important achievement. It certainly provided support for the supplementary preschool feeding programs of international, bilateral, and private voluntary agencies and for such programs as Headstart in the United States. But there were always those who questioned the lasting effects of such programs on their beneficiaries.

In this *Monograph*, Pollitt et al. now present solid evidence that the benefits of correcting early malnutrition that were considered to be small at 2 years of age could be characterized as medium to large by the time the children had become adolescents and young adults. Moreover, the effects are evident in the kinds of tests and measures known to correlate with social and economic achievement. This *Monograph* and the similar results of the follow-up (Chavez, Martinez, & Soberanes, in press) of the Mexican study should dispel these doubts. This important *Monograph* should give new motivation and impetus to efforts to avoid the tragic permanent damage of early malnutrition on many children of underprivileged families everywhere.

References

Adair, L. S., & Pollitt, E. (1985). Outcome of maternal nutritional supplementation: A comprehensive review of the Bacon Chow study. *American Journal of Clinical Nutrition,* **41,** 948–978.

Champakam, S., Srikantia, S. G., & Gopalan, C. (1968). Kwashiorkor and mental development. *American Journal of Clinical Nutrition,* **21,** 844–855.

Chavez, A., & Martinez, C. (1982). *Growing up in a developing community.* Mexico City: National Nutrition Institute.

Chavez, A., Martinez, C., & Soberanes, B. (in press). Effect of malnutrition on infant development. In N. S. Scrimshaw (Ed.), *Longitudinal community based studies of the impact of early malnutrition on child health and development.* Boston: INFDC.

Cravioto, J., & DeLicardie, E. R. (1968). Intersensory development of school-age children. In N. S. Scrimshaw & J. E. Gordon (Eds.), *Malnutrition, learning, and behavior.* Cambridge, MA: MIT Press.

Cravioto, J., DeLicardie, E. R., & Birch, H. G. (1966). Nutrition, growth and neurointegrative development: An experimental and ecologic study. *Pediatrics,* **38**(Suppl. 2, Pt. 2), 319–372.

Gerber, M., & Dean, R. F. A. (1967). The psychological changes accompanying kwashiorkor. In F. R. Wickert (Ed.), *Readings in African psychology from French language sources.* East Lansing: Michigan State University Press.

Gomez, S. F., Velasco, A. J., Ramos, G. R., Cravioto, J., & Frenk, S. (1954). Studies on malnourished children: 17. Psychological manifestations. *Boletin Médecina Hospital Infantil (Mexico),* **2,** 631–641.

Grantham-McGregor, S. M., Powell, C. A., Walker, S. P., & Himes, J. H. (1991). Nutritional supplementation, psychological stimulation and development of stunted children: The Jamaican study. *Lancet,* **338,** 1–5.

Grantham-McGregor, S. M., Stewart, M. E., & Schofield, W. N. (1980). Effect of long-term psychological stimulation on mental development of severely malnourished children. *Lancet,* **2,** 785–789.

Hoorweg, J., & Piaget, S. J. (1977). Intellectual abilities and protein-energy malnutrition: Acute malnutrition vs. chronic malnutrition. In J. Brozek (Ed.), *Behavioral effects of energy and protein deficits.* Washington, DC: U.S. Department of Health, Education, and Welfare.

Keys, L. A., Brozek, J., Henschel, A., Mickelsen, O., & Taylor, H. L. (1959). *The biology of human starvation.* Minneapolis: University of Minnesota Press.

Klein, R. E., Irwin, J., Engel, P. L., & Yarbrough, C. (1977). Malnutrition and mental development in Guatemala: An applied cross-cultural research study. In N. Warren (Ed.), *Advances in cross-cultural psychology.* New York: Academic.

McKay, H., Sinisterra, L., McKay, A., Gomez, H., & Lloreda, P. (1978). Improving cognitive ability of poorly nourished children. *Science,* **200,** 270–278.

Monckeberg, F. (1968). Effect of early marasmic malnutrition on subsequent physical and psychological development. In N. S. Scrimshaw (Ed.), *Malnutrition, learning and behavior.* Cambridge, MA: MIT Press.

Mora, J. O., Herrera, M. G., Sellers, S. G., & Ortiz, N. (1981). Nutrition, social environment and cognitive performance of disadvantaged Colombian children at three years. In *Nutrition in health and disease and international development: Symposia from the XII International Congress of Nutrition.* New York: Alan R. Liss.

Pollitt, E., & Granoff, D. (1967). Mental and motor development of Peruvian children treated for severe malnutrition. *Review of Interamerican Psychology,* **1,** 93–102.

Scrimshaw, N. S., & Gordon, J. E. (Eds.). (1968). *Malnutrition, learning, and behavior.* Cambridge, MA: MIT Press.

Sinisterra, L., McKay, A., McKay, H., Gomez, H., & Korgi, J. (1977). Response of malnourished preschool children to multidisciplinary intervention. In J. Brozek (Ed.), *Behavioral effects of energy and protein deficits.* Washington, DC: U.S. Department of Health, Education, and Welfare.

Stoch, M. B., & Smythe, P. M. (1968). Undernutrition during infancy, and subsequent brain growth and intellectual development. In N. S. Scrimshaw (Ed.), *Malnutrition, learning and behavior.* Cambridge, MA: MIT Press.

Yatkin, U. S., & McClaren, D. S. (1970). The behavioral development of infants recovering from severe malnutrition. *Journal of Mental Deficiency Research,* **14,** 25–32.

NUTRITION AND DEVELOPMENT:
CONSIDERATIONS FOR INTERVENTION

Ernesto Pollitt and Kathleen S. Gorman

The Commentaries by Theodore D. Wachs and Nevin S. Scrimshaw complement the work presented here and, for the most part, represent a natural extension of the *Monograph* discussion. Scrimshaw's discussion helps frame the current findings within a historical perspective regarding the study of malnutrition and behavior. His knowledge of the history of this topic is perhaps one of the most extensive of anyone in the field. We do take issue, however, with the rather pessimistic view evident in some of his remarks. Our understanding of human behavioral development, plasticity, and malleability leads us to a more optimistic view whereby nutritional insults are sensitive to interventions. In our view, with the exception of iodine deficiency, none of the nutritional deficiencies that represent major public health problems for a population result in an irreversible impairment of cognitive function.

The comments by Wachs flow naturally from the work in which he has been involved over the past years, in relation to both developmental theory and the significant role of malnutrition on development. At the same time, Wachs raises several issues that we feel merit further discussion. First, it is true that our measures of information processing were less stable than those of abilities and achievement. We agree that no definitive conclusions can be drawn on whether the absence of positive results regarding the nutritional intervention on information-processing variables is a result of the lack of intervention effects or the measures used.

The issue of sex differences is an interesting one. Originally, all analyses were run separately by sex. Given a very similar pattern of results, we combined the sample and tested for sex × treatment interactions. Finding no significant interactions, we then removed the interactive term and included sex as a main effect only. In a separate publication (Gorman & Pollitt, 1992), we have reported that males attain a significantly higher grade than females but that the age at which children start school is equivalent for both sexes. As the focus of the analyses in the *Monograph* was on the effects of the treatment, we did not explore all possible potential interactions. Following Ted Wach's comments, we have gone back and looked at the potential three-way interactions (treatment × sex × maximum grade attained) and found only limited evidence for differential effects based on gender. Only in two cases were the interactions significant (i.e., literacy and knowledge), and, when analyses were separated by gender, only for the knowledge test did the interactions remain significant. Similar to the results of the two-way interactions for all subjects combined, among females grade attainment was positively related to performance on the knowledge test in Atole villages, whereas there was no such association in the Fresco villages. Among males, this relation was not statistically significant.

The comments made by Wachs regarding *double buffering* raise some interesting ideas that require further clarification. We understand the results to show that, first, the Atole treatment was a buffer against the adverse effects of low SES and, second, high SES protected the subjects against the adverse effects of poor diet. Double buffering suggests to us an additive effect of Atole and SES whereby Atole subjects from the high-SES families would have outperformed the high-SES Fresco subjects. This was not the case. The results of the schooling interactions do suggest a double buffering whereby schooling and treatment combined were associated with the highest performance. Again, we would maintain that the different patterns of interactions reflect differences in variability of opportunity provided by SES and schooling.

Finally, we agree with the clarifications and additions of the model proposed by Wachs, which include the important cultural and ecological context in which behavior occurs. We would also point out that growth and activity are not necessarily independent effects and that caregiver behavior and exploration are not independent processes. The process is complex, and one could expect multiple points of interaction.

In terms of policy implications, Wachs argues that the data are strongest in supporting interventions for low-socioeconomic-status children, and we fully agree. However, not all children who benefited from the treatment were necessarily from low-SES backgrounds. Therefore, by targeting only low-SES children, the potential benefits of the nutritional intervention for other children who remain in school would be lost. These broad-range effects in the context of a rural and economically impoverished community need to be accounted for in arguments that favor feeding only the poorest of the poor. This would be an enormous disservice to children everywhere.

Interventions must be multifocal, ongoing, and available to all children in need. In this sense, we agree with Wachs in asserting the importance of nutritional aid, economic aid, and keeping *all* (our emphasis) children in school for as long as possible.

Reference

Gorman, K., & Pollitt, E. (1992). School efficiency in rural Guatemala. *International Review of Education,* **38**(5), 519–534.

CONTRIBUTORS

Ernesto Pollitt (Ph.D. 1968, Cornell University) is a psychologist and professor of human development at the Department of Pediatrics, School of Medicine, and member of the Program of International Nutrition, University of California, Davis. He is coprincipal investigator of the follow-up study reported in this *Monograph*. The main research focus of his professional career has been on the interactions between malnutrition and behavioral development in low-income countries.

Kathleen S. Gorman (Ph.D. 1987, University of Maryland) is a psychologist and research associate at the Department of Pediatrics, School of Medicine, University of California, Davis. She was the field director of the behavioral sciences component of the follow-up study. Her research work has been primarily concerned with the determinants of educational progress among rural children in Guatemala.

Patrice L. Engle (Ph.D. 1971, Stanford University) is a psychologist and chair of the Department of Psychology of the California Polytechnic Institute. She participated in both the longitudinal and the follow-up phases of the study. She has published extensively on the effects of women's work on child rearing and development in rural populations in Central American countries.

Reynaldo Martorell (Ph.D. 1973, University of Washington) is a physical anthropologist, the principal investigator of the follow-up study, and a member of the research team that conducted the longitudinal study. At the time the follow-up study began, he was a professor of nutrition at Stanford University and later became leading professor at the Division of Nutrition at Cornell University. One of the main areas of his research has been the synergistic relation of infection and physical growth and the effects of early supplementary feeding on growth and development in low-income countries.

Juan Rivera (Ph.D. 1988, Cornell University) is a nutrition epidemiologist and currently head of the Division of Nutrition and Health at the Institute of Nutrition of Central America and Panama, Guatemala City. He served as the scientific and technical coordinator of the follow-up study. One of his research interests has been the effects of nutrition supplementation in the rehabilitation of severely malnourished children.

Theodore D. Wachs (Ph.D. 1968, George Peabody College) is professor of Psychological Sciences at Purdue University. He is a member of the editorial boards of *Child Development, Developmental Psychology,* and the *International Journal of Behavioral Development.* He is the author of *The Nature of Nurture* (1992) and coeditor (with Robert Plomin) of *Conceptualization and Measurement of Organism Environment Interaction* (1991). His research interests include the study of the role of early environmental influences on development and investigating the processes whereby individual difference factors mediate relations between environment and development.

Nevin S. Scrimshaw (Ph.D. 1941, Harvard University; M.D. 1945, University of Rochester; M.P.H. 1959, Harvard University) is a clinical and public health nutritionist who founded the Institute of Nutrition of Central America and Panama (INCAP) and served for many years as head of the Department of Nutrition and Food Science at the Massachusetts Institute of Technology. He is now Institute Professor Emeritus. In 1975, he organized the World Hunger Programme for the United Nations University, Tokyo, and continues to direct its food and nutrition activities. He is the founder and president of the International Nutrition Foundation for Developing Countries (INFDC). In 1991, he was named the World Food Prize laureate. His current interests relate to the functional consequences of iron deficiency, the effects of chronic energy deficiency on developing country populations, rapid assessment procedures for the evaluation and improvement of programs of nutrition and primary health care, and nutrition, health, and demographic transition in developing countries. He is the author of over 600 publications and the author or editor of 15 books.

STATEMENT OF EDITORIAL POLICY

The *Monographs* series is intended as an outlet for major reports of developmental research that generate authoritative new findings and use these to foster a fresh and/or better-integrated perspective on some conceptually significant issue or controversy. Submissions from programmatic research projects are particularly welcome; these may consist of individually or group-authored reports of findings from some single large-scale investigation or of a sequence of experiments centering on some particular question. Multiauthored sets of independent studies that center on the same underlying question can also be appropriate; a critical requirement in such instances is that the various authors address common issues and that the contribution arising from the set as a whole be both unique and substantial. In essence, irrespective of how it may be framed, any work that contributes significant data and/or extends developmental thinking will be taken under editorial consideration.

Submissions should contain a minimum of 80 manuscript pages (including tables and references); the upper limit of 150–175 pages is much more flexible (please submit four copies; a copy of every submission and associated correspondence is deposited eventually in the archives of the SRCD). Neither membership in the Society for Research in Child Development nor affiliation with the academic discipline of psychology are relevant; the significance of the work in extending developmental theory and in contributing new empirical information is by far the most crucial consideration. Because the aim of the series is not only to advance knowledge on specialized topics but also to enhance cross-fertilization among disciplines or subfields, it is important that the links between the specific issues under study and larger questions relating to developmental processes emerge as clearly to the general reader as to specialists on the given topic.

Potential authors who may be unsure whether the manuscript they are planning would make an appropriate submission are invited to draft an outline of what they propose and send it to the Editor for assessment.

This mechanism, as well as a more detailed description of all editorial policies, evaluation processes, and format requirements, is given in the "Guidelines for the Preparation of *Monographs* Submissions," which can be obtained by writing to the Editor designate, Rachel K. Clifton, Department of Psychology, University of Massachusetts, Amherst, MA 01003.